Ursula Markham was born in Hertfordshire and brought up and educated in London. She has two sons, now in their early thirties.

She has been a practising hypnotherapist since 1979 with her own successful clinics, first in London and now in Gloucestershire.

Ursula is Principal of The Hypnothink Foundation which exists to promote research and education about the potential and power of the human mind and which runs training courses in hypnotherapy to professional level. She speaks regularly on radio and television and gives lectures and conducts workshops in Britain and overseas.

Author of more than twenty self-help books, Ursula has also produced a range of self-help cassettes dealing with a variety of topics.

She can be contacted through The Hypnothink Foundation, PO Box 66, Gloucester GL2 9YG.

HYPNOTHERAPY

A guide to improving health and well-being with hypnosis

Ursula Markham

Illustrated by
Shaun Williams

VERMILION
LONDON

First Published Macdonald Optima in 1987

1 3 5 7 9 10 8 6 4 2

This revised edition published in the United Kingdom in 1997 by
Vermilion, an imprint of Ebury Press

Random House UK Ltd
Random House
20 Vauxhall Bridge Road
London SW1V 2SA

Random House Australia (Pty) Ltd
20 Alfred Street, Milsons Point, Sydney
New South Wales 2016, Australia

Random House New Zealand Limited
18 Poland Rd, Glenfield,
Aukland 10, New Zealand

Random House South Africa (Pty) Limited
Endulini, 5A Jubilee Road, Parktown 2193, South Africa

Random House UK Limited Reg. No. 954009

A CIP catalogue record for this book is available from the British
Library.

ISBN 0 09 181519 3

Printed and bound in Great Britain by Mackays of Chatham, Plc

Papers used by Vermilion are natural, recyclable products made from
wood grown in sustainable forests.

To Philip and David
with all my love . . .

'You are never given a wish without also
being given the power to make it true.
You may have to work for it however.'

(Richard Bach, *Illusions*)

CONTENTS

INTRODUCTION   9

1. ABOUT HYPNOSIS   11
   Historical background   11
   What is hypnosis?   16
   Self-hypnosis   19
   The first consultation   20

2. YOUR QUESTIONS ANSWERED   25

3. RELAXATION AND VISUALIZATION   49
   Relaxation   49
   The benefits of relaxation   50
   Learning how to relax   53
   Practising at home   54
   The power of the imagination   55
   Visualization   57

4. SMOKING AND OBESITY   61
   Smoking   61
   Reasons for giving up   61
   Why other methods fail   64
   Why hypnotherapy works   65
   How many visits will it take?   66
   What form will the treatment take?   67
   Obesity   69
   Treating obesity   73

5. PHOBIAS   79
   What is a phobia?   79
   Treating a phobia   80

6. SOME COMMON USES OF HYPNOSIS   89
   Depression   89
   Lack of confidence   93
   Insomnia   96
   Nail-biting   97
   Stammering   98
   Blushing   100
   Infertility   100
   Impotence   102

7. PAIN AND ILLNESS   107
   Pain with a physical cause   108
   Psychosomatic pain   109
   Hypnosis and dentistry   113
   Childbirth   115
   High blood-pressure   116
   Migraine   116
   Asthma   117
   Cancer   118

8. FURTHER INFORMATION   123
   Further reading   123
   Useful addresses   125

INTRODUCTION

Hypnosis is increasingly being used to relieve and cure a wide range of disorders, from physical ailments to problems of a psychological or emotional nature. Many sufferers, however, are deterred from seeking the help of a hypnotherapist because of fear or ignorance about the concept of hypnosis itself, or because they have seen examples of theatrical hypnotism where those taking part have been made to look foolish or lacking in control.

This book attempts to set the record straight. It explains exactly what hypnosis is, and describes how, when practised by a trained and ethical therapist, it can bring great benefits to a vast number of people suffering from many different types of problems.

Hypnotherapy can help you to find the 'inner you' — the person you were really meant to be. Do you suffer from a phobia or wish to stop smoking? Are you studying for exams or eating too much? Perhaps you are being adversely affected by the stresses and pressures of twentieth-century life. To all these problems — and to many, many others — hypnosis can provide a solution.

1.
ABOUT HYPNOSIS

HISTORICAL BACKGROUND

No one is quite sure how and when hypnotism came into being, although it was certainly in use as a cure by early civilizations such as the Ancient Egyptians, Persians, Greeks and Romans.

Many people believe that Anton Mesmer (1734-1815) was the originator of modern-day hypnotism. And yet what Mesmer produced was not really hypnotism at all.

Mesmer first trained for the priesthood, but went on to study law at the University of Vienna before becoming a physician. He was convinced that magnetism could and would alleviate a large number of ailments. He achieved many 'cures' by various methods, one of which was to attach magnets to different parts of his patients' bodies. Although Mesmer believed that he was harnessing magnetic energy for therapeutic purposes, other later experts were of the opinion that the reason for the success of this process lay in the faith and trust of Mesmer's patients, and their acceptance of the value of his treatment.

Mesmer later came to Paris under the patronage of Queen Marie Antoinette, and for some time thereafter was the darling of society, being called upon to treat many members of Louis XVI's court. He was a showman who liked to surround himself with an air of mystery. He treated his patients under dimmed lights, with the air heavily perfumed and the room filled with the sound of strange music. He would wave his arms about in flamboyant fashion, making elaborate passes in the air to persuade his patients that they were in fact receiving the 'magnetic fluid' which he claimed would cure their ills. It may well have been that some of Mesmer's patients were rather suggestible; but, for whatever reason, there is no doubt that some cures were actually recorded. On reflection, however, it seems likely that any hypnotic effect achieved was accidental rather than deliberate.

Mesmer met considerable antagonism from contemporary physicians. In 1778 a French Government Commission was appointed to investigate his treatments and his alleged cures. It condemned his activities and accused him of mysticism. Forced into retirement, Mesmer went to live in Meersburg where he later died, leaving behind him his name, perpetuated in the word 'mesmerism', and the legend of a charismatic man able to effect cures, by whatever means, and to inspire a number of followers. Those followers went on to bring closer an acceptance of hypnotism as it is today.

In later years Richard Chenevix, a Fellow of the Royal Society, declared that 'the most extraordinary event in the whole history of human science is that mesmerism even could be doubted'.

The Marquis de Puységur was one of Mesmer's disciples. In the beginning he worked in much the same way as his teacher, waving his hands in the air and making ritualistic passes around the patient. It was Puységur who first discovered somnambulism. He was in the process of treating an agricultural worker for a chest complaint, making the usual passes in the air, when the man passed into what was then called 'magnetic somnambulism' — a state in which, as is shown by contemporary records, he exhibited all the classic signs of having been hypnotized. Medical authorities of the time were a little more inclined to approve this manner of achieving a hypnotic state than they were to accept the theory of magnetism.

In the early nineteenth century, Dr John Elliotson, Professor of Medicine at the new University College in London and President of the Royal Medical Society, used hypnosis when treating his patients. During his time at University College Hospital he was said to have used hypnosis many times to enable him to perform painless surgery. However, this was stopped in 1838, when the hospital authorities passed a resolution forbidding it. Elliotson, one of the first men to use the stethoscope, was sufficiently respected, though, to be able to give a more substantial basis to the idea that hypnosis was a genuine form of treatment, and not just some theatrical mumbo-jumbo employed by charlatans. One of the great influences on Elliotson was Franz Joseph Gall (the father of phrenology) who strongly supported the theory that the mind is often responsible for the ailments of the body.

James Braid (1795-1860) was the first man to proclaim that the hypnotic state could be achieved just as well and just as efficiently without the use of magnets. He would ask his patient to gaze at a single point of concentration while the relevant suggestions were being made. He was also responsible for coining the word 'hypnotism', from the Greek word *hypnos* meaning 'sleep'.

Braid was not in the habit of making ridiculous claims for hypnosis and what it could achieve. This restraint on his part may have been why he was the first of its supporters to be taken really seriously. He said: 'We have acquired an important curative agency for a certain class of diseases', and went on to add, 'I by no means wish to hold it up as a universal remedy' (James Braid, *The Rationale of Nervous Sleep Considered in Relation to Animal Magnetism*, 1843). In 1846 he went on to publish *The Power of the Mind over the Body*.

James Esdaile (1808-59) was a Scottish-born doctor who worked for much of his life in India. In 1852 he published a record of surgical operations which he claimed to have performed painlessly, using what he called 'mesmeric anaesthesia'. At that time — as now — hypnosis was also being used in dentistry.

Dr Liébault (1823-1904) and Dr Bernheim were both eminent professors at the University of Nancy in France. They did not believe that any specific neurological mechanism was involved in hypnosis, but felt that patients would enter the hypnotic state provided the suggestion had been planted firmly enough in their minds.

Liébault had been a country doctor, and had found in his practice that verbal suggestion could make an extremely effective contribution to treatment. He later went on to found the Nancy School of Hypnotism.

Another Frenchman, Professor Charcot (1825-93), heard of the theories of James Braid. Like him, Charcot believed that hypnosis could be readily induced if the patient was prepared to accept the necessary suggestion, and that no artificial means was necessary.

Charcot was an eminent man who worked with Pierre Janet, Sigmund Freud and Alfred Binet (the inventor of the IQ test). These men formed such a distinguished and respectable group that it could no longer be claimed that hypnosis was merely the tool of cranks and eccentrics. Indeed Charcot was later responsible for founding the

Salpêtrière School of Hypnotism.

Pierre Janet was a pupil of Charcot and afterwards went on to work with him. He postulated the theory that hypnosis meant that one part of the mind was functioning entirely independently of the rest. Janet found that patients with neurotic disorders often had complete gaps in their memories — they would forget incidents which had been painful or distressing. Under hypnosis those forgotten incidents could be recalled, and this enabled the patients to understand the cause of their problems and therefore to progress towards overcoming them.

Sigmund Freud (1856-1939) studied with Liébault and Bernheim at Nancy, and with Charcot at Salpêtrière. He also worked with Pierre Janet. Freud used hypnosis to investigate the subconscious mind. He was one of the first to advance the theory that revealing the cause of an anxiety is an essential first step along the path to a cure. What he did not fully appreciate was that another essential for success is cooperation from the patient.

WHAT FREUD DID NOT FULLY APPRECIATE WAS THAT ANOTHER ESSENTIAL FOR SUCCESS IS COOPERATION FROM THE PATIENT HIMSELF.

When, in some cases, this cooperation was lacking and the expected cure did not take place, Freud became disillusioned and abandoned hypnosis in favour of psychoanalysis — where the therapist has to be a patient and attentive listener rather than an active instigator of a specific process. Psychoanalysis did and does produce results. However, whereas hypnosis can bring relief in a relatively short time, psychoanalysis takes much longer — sometimes several years.

The efforts of the originators of what can be called the 'golden age' of hypnosis during the last part of the nineteenth century were largely forgotten as their work was replaced by psychoanalysis and psychotherapy. It is only in recent years that hypnosis has come back into favour and that the public, together with enlightened members of the medical profession, have begun to appreciate its true value and effectiveness.

WHAT IS HYPNOSIS?

Hypnosis is an altered state of awareness. It is that very special link which forms a bridge between the mind and the body.

Much harm has been done to the concept of hypnosis as a therapy by performances of theatrical hypnotism. That is not to imply that I am against hypnotism used in this way (although it is not something I practise myself), but it should be seen for what it is — a form of entertainment with audience participation. Any volunteers who go on stage during such a performance and take part in the show know precisely what they are letting themselves in for. What I do find sad is that such performances shake the confidence of so many people in the use of hypnosis as a genuine and very effective therapy.

Stage hypnotism
Theatrical hypnotism must be put in its correct perspective. During the course of a performance the hypnotist will ask all the members of the audience —

sometimes as many as several hundred people — to take part in a simple test. Most frequently, this involves clasping the hands above the head while the hypnotist tells them that they will be unable to unclasp them again. A certain number will in fact be unable to part their hands, and the entertainer will ask those people to join him or her on stage.

Sometimes as many as 50 or 60 people will present themselves on the stage; the performer then puts them through a number of small tests. These are designed to indicate which of the volunteers are the real extroverts — those who want so much to be part of the performance that they are, in fact, hypnotizing themselves. You will usually find, at the end of the selection period, that about ten members of the audience remain on stage, and it is with this small number that the hypnotist will work.

If you bear in mind that the first rule of hypnosis is that no one can be hypnotized if he or she does not wish to be, you will see that those volunteers who remain at the end of the final test are the ones who desperately want to be part of the show. They are people who, if they were not performing on the theatre's stage, would probably be the 'life and soul of the party' elsewhere. Any original volunteers who may have gone forward just out of a sense of bravado, or because they were encouraged by friends, will not satisfactorily complete the rapid series of tests while there is any apprehension in their minds. They will merely be thanked and asked to return to their seats.

So those among you — and be assured that you are in the majority — who would be filled with horror at the thought of looking foolish in front of an audience of hundreds can rest assured that, even had you been persuaded to volunteer in the first place, you would never have allowed yourself to do anything which you did not really want to do.

Clinical hypnosis
Hypnosis can be used with great effect to cure a wide range of ills.

Hypnosis itself is a state of heightened suggestibility. It is a sleeplike condition where all the physiological reflexes (such as knee-jerking) are still present. To be hypnotized is like being in a pleasantly relaxed and drowsy state. In this state, the suggestions of the therapist can reach your subconscious mind while the conscious mind remains relaxed.

Hypnosis involves complete mental and physical relaxation, and is brought about by cooperation between the knowledge and technique of the therapist and the mind and imagination of the subject. That cooperation is very important, because it underlines the fact that to become hypnotized is not to be in a purely passive state. You have to play your part too. For example, if the therapist tells you that your arms are growing heavy, you have to use your imagination and allow this to happen. The hypnotherapist is not in possession of a magic wand which will *make* your arms grow heavy.

Very many people find the word 'trance' frightening. They immediately think they are going to fall under another's influence and will have no control over their own thoughts and actions. In fact, what you feel is pleasantly warm, comfortable and relaxed — and quite capable of hearing and understanding every word said to you.

All your skills and abilities are filed away in the back of your mind. Hypnosis helps you to rediscover the natural aptitudes which are yours already. You will not need to learn anything new; all that is required is a re-adjustment and re-arrangement of your existing talents.

Hypnosis itself does not cure anything. It is simply a state of sensitivity and increased awareness which allows the cure to take place. During hypnosis the autonomic nervous system is receptive, and since the subconscious is part of the nervous system, it can be reached by the words and suggestions of the therapist without the interference of the patient's conscious mind. This makes it possible to get to the root of deep-seated emotional problems, and to give the patient the tools with which to overcome them.

Many people think that they are going to be under the influence of another person and that they will have no control over their own thoughts and actions

SELF-HYPNOSIS

It has been said that all hypnosis is self-hypnosis, and to a great extent this is true. Patients are only hypnotized because they allow themselves to be, and because they cooperate with the therapist to make it happen. Nonetheless, it is often the very presence of the therapist which gives patients the confidence to allow this to happen in the first place.

There are many occasions when it is necessary to teach patients self-hypnosis, so they can practise it on their own, in their own home and their own time. It is an essential part of continuing treatment. You would not expect to reach the height of physical fitness by visiting a gymnasium just once a fortnight. In the same way, although you will be greatly helped by the hypnotherapist when you see him or her weekly, fortnightly or monthly as the case may be, the results will come much more quickly and easily if you do your own 'homework'.

There are certain cases where the teaching of self-hypnosis is essential. If a pregnant woman goes into labour at three in the morning, she will find it extremely difficult to get hold of her hypnotherapist. However, if she has been taught self-hypnosis, so that she is aware of precisely what to do and how to do it, she will be able to control the whole situation.

If an asthmatic felt that breathing was becoming difficult yet had to wait to contact the therapist and for him or her to arrive, the difficulty could well have developed into a full-scale attack. But a patient who has been taught self-hypnosis will be able to control the situation alone. Apart from the fact that there are very few people who will want to continue to pay a therapist for years and years, how much more rewarding and confidence-building it is to know that you yourself have the ability to deal with a situation which may have caused you anxiety in the past.

Self-hypnosis is a natural extension of the treatment you receive from your therapist. Once you have been successfully hypnotized, and are aware of what being hypnotized feels like and the beneficial effects which follow, you will be taught just how to achieve that feeling and those effects for yourself. Although you will have to practise the technique on your own at home, your therapist will be able to help you should you experience any initial difficulties.

THE FIRST CONSULTATION

So you have made up your mind that hypnotherapy may well be the answer to your problems. What exactly will happen when you are hypnotized? What will it feel like?

The first thing to understand is what you will *not* be. You will not be 'unconscious' or 'in the power' of the

therapist. At all times you will be able to think, you will
hear precisely what is going on, and your mind will be in
control of the situation. If the hypnotherapist were to
suggest anything to you which you found objectionable,
you would wake up. Your ego remains the same whether
you are hypnotized or not. There is no way in which you
are going to become more weak-willed just because you
have been hypnotized.

The hypnotherapist will probably spend a good deal of
time just talking to you before actually hypnotizing you.
This discussion time is extremely important in order to set
your mind at rest about any aspect which bothers you. It
is also an opportunity for the therapist to explain the way
in which he or she works; all hypnotherapists do not
induce the hypnotic state in precisely the same way.

In my own case, I also take the time to prove to patients
whether or not they are good subjects for hypnosis. This
little test-session only takes five or ten minutes, but it
achieves a great deal. For one thing it proves to patients
beyond any doubt that they are sufficiently good subjects;
for another, it gives them a brief taste of what it feels like
to be hypnotized so that, when it is time to treat them
therapeutically, their mind is not kept too alert wondering
just what I am going to do next. Even if it is not normal
practice, any therapist should be willing to do the same if
you ask.

When you are in the hypnotic state you should feel
completely relaxed, mentally and physically. The closest
analogy, perhaps, is the feeling of being warm and snug in
your bed at night, but not actually asleep. If someone were
then to come into your room who had every right to be
there, you might well be aware that they had come in but
you would not necessarily move or do anything about it.
If, however, someone entered who should not be there,
your mind would be awake and alert instantly. In just the
same way, as long as you feel you have confidence in your
therapist and as long as you wish to be hypnotized, you
will remain in that relaxed and drowsy state. In any
emergency, however, you would immediately be fully

awake and in complete control of your senses and your reactions.

When you allow yourself to be hypnotized your mind will be 'switched off', and the stresses of everyday life will seem far away. There is a sense of double awareness, in which you allow your mind to drift into a distant warm and comfortable world while, at the same time, you are quite aware of where you are and of the chair on which you are sitting.

If you are hypnotized several times you may find that you allow yourself to drift a little deeper on each occasion. You will still be aware of everything around you, but as your confidence in hypnotherapy — and in particular in the hypnotherapist — grows, so your conscious mind will be willing to surrender more and more.

When you are woken up after the session you should feel pleasantly relaxed. You will not be left in some somnambulistic state, not fully in control of your faculties. There is no such thing as being 'half-hypnotized'. You are either in the hypnotic state or you are not. So, although you should be feeling more tension-free than usual, you will be completely in command of every situation.

...YOU WILL NOT BE LEFT IN SOME SOMNAMBULISTIC STATE...

The therapist can induce the hypnotic state in one of several ways. Basically these techniques fall into two main categories:

Vocal suggestion: In this case the hypnotist will talk to you, gently and calmly, suggesting that your body will become heavier and more relaxed and that your mind will be peaceful and quiet. Often you will be asked to close your eyes — this aids concentration and avoids the distraction of being in a strange room. Sometimes the therapist will use pleasant mental images to help the process along. You may be asked to imagine taking an enjoyable walk along a country lane, by the seashore or in a garden. In some cases there will be gentle and meditative music in the background.

Fascination: This can take various forms. Sometimes you may be asked to stare at a point on the ceiling above your head, or at a pinpoint of light, while the hypnotist speaks to you. As they speak you will feel yourself becoming drowsy until you need to close your eyes and just listen to the voice. You may be asked to concentrate on a hypnotic spiral disc such as the one illustrated below. Once again the therapist will speak to you, gently inducing a feeling of relaxation and drowsiness until you close your eyes and just listen to the voice.

Having induced in you a pleasantly relaxed hypnotic state, the therapist will continue with the treatment. The main aim is to put into your subconscious mind the positive suggestions which will enable you to overcome your own particular problem. At all times you will hear everything and understand precisely what is being said to you.

At the end of the session the hypnotherapist will usually either leave you with some 'homework' to do before the next visit (this will normally take the form of practising for yourself something which has been given to you as a post-hypnotic suggestion); or if this is to be your only session, and you are considered suitable, you may be taught self-hypnosis so that you can continue the therapy for yourself.

Once the session is at an end, you should be feeling much more relaxed and in a positive state of mind. Whether or not further sessions are needed will depend very much on your susceptibility to hypnosis, and on the opinion of the therapist.

2.
YOUR QUESTIONS ANSWERED

Can anyone be hypnotized?
With a very few exceptions, anyone who wants to be hypnotized can be. The opposite is also true — if you do not want to be hypnotized you will not be. Hypnosis is essentially a matter of cooperation between the therapist and the patient, not some form of power the therapist possesses which will compel the patient to submit to his or her will. Reputable hypnotherapists will only try to help you to achieve that which you want, not force you to do something *they* wish.

However, someone with a history of epilepsy should never be hypnotized. Even if the situation is well under control with drugs, the altered state of hypnosis could actually (although would not necessarily) induce an epileptic fit.

Since cooperation is such an important factor in hypnosis, those who are unable to cooperate will also be unable to enter the hypnotic state. There are really three main categories of people to whom this applies:
* those who are mentally deficient in some way which makes cooperation impossible;
* children under the age of five years;
* those who are under the influence of alcohol — perhaps we might say that such people are temporarily mentally deficient!

There are two other types of people that I would not choose to treat by hypnosis. I would not consider as a patient anyone who had a severe drink problem, unless I had a residential clinic where the patient could remain for several weeks. The reason is that no one is cured of a problem in just one session. If a patient had to leave the clinic and then go home past off-licences and public houses, the tension set up by the conflict between wanting to stop drinking and the temptation to drink would probably make the problem worse rather than better.

Neither would I accept as a patient anyone who used hard drugs. I have neither the knowledge required nor the access to the drugs needed during withdrawal to treat these people properly, so I usually send them to a local clinic which specializes in such treatment.

Is there an ideal hypnotic subject?
The best hypnotic subject is the person who:
- really wants to be hypnotized;
- is willing to cooperate fully with the therapist rather than to sit back and let it happen;
- has a good visual imagination;
- is intelligent enough to understand the explanations given and to play a full part in the proceedings.

It is a fallacy to think that it is only less intelligent people who make good hypnotic subjects — the reverse is actually true. Equally those who state emphatically, 'I am far too strong-willed to be hypnotized', are not correct. A strong will can be used in either a positive or a negative way, and those who declare on the one hand that they want to be hypnotized and, on the other, that their 'strong will' does not permit this, are in fact fooling themselves. What they are really saying is: 'I do not want to be hypnotized so I will use all the strength of will I possess to ensure that it does not happen.'

This, of course, is their right. No reputable therapist would ever force them to do anything they did not wish to do. They should, however, be honest with themselves and admit that they are refusing to *allow* themselves to be hypnotized. Then perhaps they should ask why they prefer to hide behind their problems rather than be helped to overcome them.

Will I be unconscious?

At all times during the course of hypnotic treatment you will be able to hear and to think. And this is very important. You are a person with a mind and a will of your own; it is only right that you should know and understand what is being said to you. In addition, having established that hypnosis entails cooperation, how could you cooperate with the therapist if you did not know on a conscious level what was being said to you?

Many people are worried by stage hypnosis and the fact that the subjects, many of whom become ridiculous during the course of the performance, seem to have no knowledge and no recollection of anything around them. Stage hypnosis is a completely different matter and, as mentioned on page 17, those who volunteer to go on stage during the course of a hypnotic show know precisely what they are letting themselves in for.

The type of person who would normally be shocked and distressed about taking part in such a performance would not dream of volunteering in the first place. Any who do take part usually thoroughly enjoy the experience. It is their moment of stardom, of having the lights and the attention of the audience focused upon them — and they love it. But then, such people are mostly extroverts in any case, likely to enter talent competitions and be 'good for a laugh'.

The unfortunate part about stage hypnosis is that it often frightens away those people who could really benefit from hypnotherapy, but who are afraid of losing control. However, when consulting a hypnotherapist, this will not happen. You will always know exactly what is going on; and if at any time the therapist were to say something which you found objectionable, you would wake up.

Sarah was a patient of mine. A young woman of 24, she had a four-month-old baby whom she brought with her

when she came for treatment. She would feed the baby
before she came and then put him in another room. On the
only occasion the baby woke and cried, Sarah emerged
from the hypnotic state immediately. Ordinary noises
inside or outside the building never bothered her; they did
not matter enough to her to disturb her. But the sound of
her baby crying was far more important to her than her
treatment and so she woke up completely. In the same
way, if there were a real emergency — a fire for example
— your mind would take complete control and bring you
to a state of full alertness to cope with the situation.

What do I have to do?
There is only one thing you will be asked to do, and that is
to cooperate with the hypnotherapist. You will usually lie
on a couch or sit in a comfortable chair, and you will be
guided into the hypnotic state by the voice and the words
of the therapist. They would normally begin by leading
you into a state of relaxation, physical, mental and
emotional, and this can only be pleasant — and beneficial.

Sometimes it's necessary to ask a patient to speak
during the course of a session but, in that case, a
reputable therapist would have asked permission first,
before starting the session, and would have explained
exactly why it was necessary. Even then, you would be
aware of what you were saying and, should you have any
dark and deadly secrets, they would remain so. You will
never say anything which you are determined not to say.
However, it is usually in your best interests to speak
openly, particularly if you are being regressed to an earlier
period in your life in order to discover the cause of a
present-day problem.

Are there any side-effects?
The answer to that question is a very resounding 'yes'.
But the side-effects are all good ones!

From the very first time you are hypnotized, you will
find that you are better able to relax — and this can only
be good for you. Many of the problems we face today arise

out of tension, stress, anxiety ... Imagine how wonderful it would be to relax at will — to shut out, even if only temporarily, the problems of the world, and thereby lessen their damaging effect on your health.

Relaxation itself will not solve the particular problems which surround you. What it will do is to change the effect those problems have on you, and therefore the way you cope with them. In addition, learning to relax will make you far less likely to suffer from strokes, heart-attacks or other stress-related illnesses.

Another side-effect of hypnosis is that you are likely to find that you fall asleep much more easily, and that your sleep is better and deeper than before. Many of my patients — who may have come to me for any number of reasons — have told me that they sleep a great deal better than they did before being hypnotized, and that they do so without recourse to the pills or drugs they had previously been taking.

What does it feel like?
Many people are surprised to discover that they are going to feel anything at all while under hypnosis. The impression has been firmly planted in their minds that they will be 'unconscious', and will know nothing at all about what is going on.

In fact, hypnosis is a very pleasant state. You will feel warm, comfortable and relaxed. You will be aware of your surroundings, aware of the voice of the hypnotherapist, aware perhaps of a dog barking somewhere in the distance. But because none of these things disturbs you, and because you have chosen to allow yourself to be hypnotized, you will remain calm and relaxed and ready to absorb the suggestions which the therapist will make — those which are designed to help you to overcome your problems and improve your life.

Can I eat and drink beforehand?
Eating and drinking in moderation will not affect the hypnotic session one way or the other. It is better,

however, not to consume a huge meal immediately before the session, because the possible feelings of discomfort might impede your ability to relax. Equally, you should not be really hungry when you are hypnotized as this, too, could prevent you from cooperating fully with the therapist — part of you would be working out how long it would be before the next meal!

As far as drink is concerned, I prefer my patients not to have had alcohol immediately before a session. Even a little is enough to limit real concentration — and the patient has to concentrate on what the therapist is saying; and a larger quantity of alcohol would probably make you relax so completely that you would fall asleep and not have any knowledge of what was happening during the session. That would be a waste, not only of the therapist's time, but of your money.

So, moderation in all things. There is no harm in having lunch at one o'clock and then a hypnotic session at two, provided that the meal was light and preferably unaccompanied by alcohol.

What would happen if no one woke me up?

Or, as one nervous patient put it: 'Suppose you hypnotized me and then dropped dead before you woke me up again.' Even if such an event were to happen — and naturally I hope that it never will; it is certainly statistically unlikely — you would merely progress from hypnotic relaxation into a light sleep. You would probably doze for anything from 10 to 20 minutes, and then wake up again completely naturally with no ill effects at all.

The same question arises with the use of hypnotic cassettes. A tape could break; a cassette player could cease to function. In this event the same thing would happen, and the hypnotized subject would continue to sleep lightly for a while and then wake up.

Should I stop having medical treatment or taking pills?

The fact that you might be having medical treatment

would not in itself affect your suitability as a hypnotic subject. As already mentioned, if you are an epileptic then hypnotic treatment should never be undertaken, even if the condition appears to be well under control. But there is no other condition or form of medical treatment which would prevent you from being an excellent subject for hypnosis. The reverse is equally true; hypnotic treatment cannot nullify any other medical assistance you might be receiving.

Indeed, the two forms of treatment often work hand in hand. When Andrea first came to see me, she was taking a very high dose of the tranquillizer Valium every day. Her doctor was aware that she was consulting me and, although he did not think that hypnosis could help her, he knew that no harm could be done to her. Far from being unable to help, however, hypnosis gradually enabled Andrea to reduce her daily intake of tranquillizers until she could cope without them altogether. (I later received a charming letter of approval from the doctor concerned.)

Hypnosis is not an immediate substitute for pills or tablets. But it is very often the case that, by treating the deep-seated problem — especially when this comes under the heading of an anxiety-related condition — hypnosis can make the tablets redundant. However, I would never tell any patient to give up the medication prescribed and to have a course of hypnosis instead. The two forms of aid work very well in partnership, especially in the early days of treatment.

What if my visual imagination is not good?

Your imagination is possibly one of the greatest gifts you possess. It certainly repays proper use, and is often vital in the success of hypnotherapy. Many people insist that their visual imagination is not good, but it is a proven fact that the only people who are unable to 'see' clearly in their minds are those who were born blind. Others may lose the ability through lack of practice, but all children who are able to see are also able to imagine — and to imagine clearly.

31

Sadly, all too often, in this practical world of ours, imagination is driven out of a child. How many times have you heard a parent or teacher tell a child to 'concentrate on what I am saying', or to 'stop daydreaming and pay attention'. The saying which tells us that 'the dreamers of today are the doers of tomorrow' is very apt and often forgotten.

Suppose you are one of those people who feels that they do not have a good visual imagination — what can you do about it? The answer is quite simple. With a little practice on your part you can re-develop that ability quite quickly, and it will soon be as good as ever. There is a simple routine that will help you:

1. Take any ordinary, everyday object — a cup, a book, a chair. Sit for a few moments and look at that object. Really look at it. It is not enough just to think 'Oh, yes, that is a cup', and leave it at that. Study the shape, the colour, the texture of the object you have selected. Now close your eyes and 'see' that same object in your mind — and see it in as much detail as possible. If you have any difficulty in doing this, just open your eyes for a moment and look again at the object. Then close your eyes and repeat the whole process.

2. Once you are able to visualize a single object, do exactly the same thing with a group of three or four objects. Study them closely and then close your eyes and 'see' them again in the greatest possible detail.

3. Now try precisely the same technique — but with a more abstract image. Select a memory — some place where you have been in the recent or distant past. You do not have to imagine actual events unless you wish to, but in your mind try to see the place in as much detail as possible. Once you are able to do this successfully, you can never again claim that you do not have a visual imagination.

Naturally, you should not expect to be able to achieve all this in one go. Like any other muscle which has grown

Take any ordinary everyday object — a cup, a book, a chair. Sit for a few moments and look at that object. Really look at it. Study it's shape, colour and texture.

Now close your eyes and 'see' that same object in your mind — and see it in as much detail as possible ...

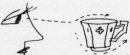

If you have any difficulty in doing this, just open your eyes for a few moments and look again at the object you have chosen.

Then close your eyes and repeat the whole process.

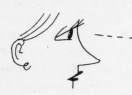

Once you are able to visualise a single object, do exactly the same thing with a group of 3 or 4 objects. Study them closely and then close your eyes and see them in the greatest possible detail.

Now try precisely the same technique — but with a more abstract image. Select a memory — some place where you have been in the recent or distant past. (You do not have to imagine actual events unless you wish to, but try to see in your mind the place and to see it in as much detail as possible.)

HOW TO DEVELOP GOOD VISUAL IMAGINATION

weak through lack of use, the 'muscle' of your imagination needs repeated and constant training. If you decided to run a marathon, you would not dream of going out just once to jog around the block, and then expect to be fit enough to run the required 26 miles. You would practise daily, building up your muscles gradually until you were as fit as you possibly could be. Do just the same with your imagination. If you have difficulty in picturing images, then take it slowly, day by day, until your confidence in that once-possessed ability returns.

Can hypnosis relieve pain?

Hypnosis is very effective in the relief of pain, but this is an area where therapists have to tread with extreme caution. We need to know just why the pain is there in the first place. It is actually comparatively easy to remove pain by hypnosis, but pain is often there for a reason. It is the body's early warning system and, as such, should not be ignored.

A seemingly simple backache may be merely the result of tiredness or tension. It could also mean that the patient has something wrong with the spine — or even is suffering from a kidney disease. I never agree merely to remove pain without either speaking to, or receiving a letter from, the patient's doctor telling me one of the following:

- the cause of the pain is known and is being treated;
- the pain appears to be psychosomatic; that is, there seems to be no *physical* reason for it;
- the patient is suffering from some stress-related condition which could be helped by hypnosis.

What sort of clothes should I wear?

There are no special rules about which clothes are most suitable for a hypnotic session. The keyword is comfort. The more comfortable you are, the easier it will be for you to relax. It is not advisable, therefore, to wear garments which are extremely tight or restricting; nor should you wear shoes which pinch — although many patients, in fact, remove their shoes when being hypnotized. And for women in particular, that often goes a long way towards making them at once feel more comfortable.

Will I have to relive distressing experiences?

In many instances it is not necessary to take a patient back to an earlier period in life at all. If patients want to give up smoking, for example, or to stop biting their nails, there is no need at all for them to experience again just why they began to do these things in the first place. It is sufficient to know that they want to stop.

In other cases, it can be of great value to go back in time, to expose some traumatic event which may have been long forgotten but which is still affecting the life and well-being of the patient. One thing I would never do, however, is to regress a patient without his or her express permission, and without explaining precisely what is involved. If the patient is determined, for whatever reason, not to undergo any form of regression, then no ethical hypnotherapist would dream of insisting on it. What I have quite often found is that patients will begin by refusing even to consider such a form of treatment, but after two or three sessions of hypnotherapy, during which time they have built up their confidence in me and in hypnosis in general, they will actually suggest regression themselves.

When Joanna first came to see me, it was to ask for my help in relieving the tension which seemed to surround her every day of her life. She is an intelligent woman with a successful career, and although she had the petty, everyday worries which plague all of us, she could find no real reason for the continual anxiety she felt. This in turn only served to increase her frustration with herself — she felt she was acting like a fool but could not help it — and so the stress and tension increased too.

After a couple of sessions during which she learned to relax mentally and physically, and was beginning to cope with the tension which had become so much part of her life, Joanna told me that she felt that there was some sort of emotional block which was affecting her and her attitude to those around her — particularly her husband. She said that she did, in fact, love her husband, but could often hear herself being very harsh and bitter towards him. This made her angry with herself, the tension increased and so did her harshness. She desperately wanted to get off this treadmill as she did not want to destroy her marriage.

I asked Joanna whether she thought that there was anything in her earlier life which could have caused this attitude towards her husband — perhaps something in her relationship with her mother or, more particularly, her father. She told me that she could think of nothing; in fact she had had a relatively happy and comfortable childhood. But she could not remember much about the period when she was between 12 and 14 years old. This is always significant. If someone has a blank spot like that in their memory of childhood or adolescence, it often means that they have shut out a particular memory — something which caused them distress at the time, and which they have subconsciously chosen to 'forget'.

Joanna was an intelligent and educated woman, and she could understand the theory that if hypnosis could take her back to the age she had 'forgotten', she might well uncover the reason for her present-day stress, and for her attitude towards her husband. Because of this understanding on her part, she was quite willing for me to regress her.

I took her back gently through her teenage years until we reached the age of 12½. At that point her whole attitude changed. She told me that her Uncle Harry, her father's brother and a frequent visitor to their home, had tried to assault her when he had found himself alone with her. Although sexual relations had not in fact happened, the event had been enough to upset the young girl. She had never told anyone what had taken place, knowing that her father was extremely fond of his brother. Uncle Harry had continued to visit frequently — although the incident was never repeated — until just after Joanna's 14th birthday, when his business commitments had taken him to another part of the country.

When I brought Joanna back again to the present she could remember everything which had happened and was astonished, as she had affectionate memories of her Uncle Harry, and absolutely no recollection of the incident which had been blocked from her conscious mind. She was well able to understand how the occurrence could have affected her as a young girl but, looking at it now through the eyes of a mature woman, she was prepared to forgive and forget it.

Of course, what she had been doing was blaming men in general, and her husband in particular, for that early assault: coming to terms with this eventually enabled her to change her attitude towards her husband. It also meant that she could now understand the reason for her earlier antagonism. Understanding a situation, of course, does not necessarily put an end to it. But, in this particular case, it did serve to dissipate the anger Joanna felt towards herself. This in turn relieved much of her inner tension.

Sometimes, although not in every case, the things which distressed us when we were young are not nearly as upsetting when seen through adult eyes. So regression can serve a significant purpose as part of hypnotic treatment. Nonetheless, although such a form of treatment may be recommended, no ethical therapist would ever regress a patient who did not want it.

Some people are frightened that they will be made to relive pain, whether emotional or physical, which they have suffered in the past. There are, however, techniques for avoiding this. It is always possible for the hypnotherapist to see when patients are approaching some trauma of this sort during the course of treatment; the breathing changes, as does the eye movement. What I then do is to transfer the image to one on a 'cinema screen' in the patients' minds, rather than allowing them actually to relive the experience.

If you were to see a home movie of yourself as a child falling over and grazing both knees, you might well see the child on the screen crying; you could even see that the knees were bleeding. But the adult watching that movie would not actually feel the pain or want to cry. If, during a

TO AVOID RELIVING PAIN THE IMAGE IS TRANSFERRED TO ONE ON A 'CINEMA SCREEN' IN THE PATIENT'S MIND.

hypnotic session, I feel that you are about to enter an extremely traumatic period of your life while being regressed, I produce just this effect. In other words, you will see and understand what is happening, but you will not feel any physical pain or any distress. Used in this way, the regression can prove to be just as beneficial as Joanna's was to her.

Will I need to do anything between sessions?

I usually send patients away with some 'homework' to do between visits. They will not necessarily have to hypnotize themselves — although some are taught self-hypnosis — but they will be given post-hypnotic suggestions (which they will hear and understand) outlining what I would like them to do to help themselves. In most cases this will entail spending about 15 minutes a day, using a combination of relaxation techniques and visualization to reinforce the treatment I have given during the session.

As well as suggesting to them during the hypnotic session itself that they will practise in this way, I always discuss the subject in detail with patients before they leave, so that they know exactly what I am doing and why. I do not believe in a 'mystique' of hypnotherapy. Hypnosis only succeeds when it combines learned techniques with the intelligence of the patients themselves, plus their own desire to be helped.

I generally suggest to patients that they should practise their technique in what I call the 'twilight' time at night — that drowsy space which lies between being awake and falling asleep. Sometimes patients will telephone to say that they have been so relaxed during the course of practising that they have fallen asleep, and never reached the end of the visualization. This, in fact, does not matter at all. Once a suggestion has been given under hypnosis, it has reached the subconscious as well as the conscious mind; the process will therefore continue even if the conscious mind 'shuts down' when the patient falls asleep. Think of it as a cassette which you have decided to play. As long as you put the tape in the machine and start the mechanism, it will continue to play until it comes to the end — even if you decide to leave the room.

The work that you do for yourself between visits is of vital importance. For one thing, it shows commitment on your part — that you are prepared to assist the therapist to help you, and are not merely sitting back and waiting for the wave of some hypnotic magic wand. In addition, hypnosis makes it possible for positive suggestions to reach your subconscious mind, and to give you the confidence to set your sights high. How much more satisfactory it is to develop and improve that process by bringing into action your conscious mind, too. The harder you work between hypnotherapy sessions, the sooner you will achieve whatever it is that you have set out to do, and the more confident you will be about yourself and your own ability.

What problems can be helped by hypnotherapy?

Any problem which can be put there by your mind can also be taken away by your mind. If you break a bone in your leg, it will take a certain amount of time to heal, and there is very little that you can do, on a mental level, to alter that period of time. So hypnosis will not really help.

Most problems today, however, have an emotional or mental cause rather than a physical one. Many things, from nail-biting to cancer, can have an emotional base and so be helped by hypnosis. Later chapters outline the main problems which hypnosis can help to overcome — and I am sure that there are many you had never thought of as having an emotional cause.

How long does each session last?

It is very difficult to give a hard and fast answer to this question. Obviously people and their problems vary considerably. As a general guide, I normally find that the initial consultation lasts for about an hour. Much of this time will be spent talking to the patient about his or her problem. When it is relevant, I like the patient to make suggestions as to why the problem may have arisen in the first place — and why it has continued so long that help is now needed to dispose of it. Quite often, of course, when someone comes to my consulting room to tell me about what is believed to be the *problem*, what is actually described is the *symptom*. The problem may be far more deep-rooted than is imagined.

During the initial consultation I also discuss hypnotherapy in general, how and why it works, and what methods I use. And of course I conduct the five-minute test mentioned in the previous chapter (page 21). Only after the patient's mind has been set at rest about hypnosis and how it works will I actually begin treatment.

Subsequent visits are sometimes shorter, sometimes longer. If I am treating someone to prevent them from smoking or to overcome obesity, for example, and if all appears to be going well, then the session may last no more than half-an-hour. Naturally, should any problems arise, even in what appears to be a straightforward case, then these will have to be discussed and the time taken will accordingly be longer.

For patients suffering from something like depressive illness, however, every session could last for a full hour, since far more discussion is needed, as well as a deeper relaxation therapy, before we can even consider continuing to the next part of that session's treatment.

How many sessions will I need?

This is a difficult question to answer with any degree of accuracy. Generalizations are really not possible. For example, I normally tell a smoker who wishes to give up the habit to expect to have to come and see me three or four times at weekly intervals. However there are always patients like Emma, a woman of 63, who was able to stop completely after coming to see me just once. She has never smoked since. So it may be that one visit only will be necessary, but this is unusual. On the other hand, there are also those who need more than the expected three or four visits — but these too are in a minority. By far the greatest number of patients become non-smokers within the estimated time — three to four visits.

With obesity patients, the number of visits depends on the amount of weight they need to lose. This also affects the frequency of their visits. The normal procedure is to see overweight patients one week after their initial visit. If they are doing well, then I would expect to see them fortnightly for a month or so. After that, if there is still weight to lose, I would suggest they come and see me once a month until they reach the desired weight. However, they can always come for an extra visit or two if problems arise.

A pregnant woman who wished to alleviate the pain and discomfort of childbirth would only need to come for long enough to be taught self-hypnosis. This is essential in such cases, since the therapist is unlikely to be present at the actual birth and so the mother must be able to hypnotize herself. One of my patients, Samantha, who already had two children (having had them 'the hard way' as she put it) was taught self-hypnosis in preparation for the birth of her third child. She had a completely pain-free labour and wrote to me soon afterwards: 'I was lying there reading a Catherine Cookson novel while everything was happening. If only I had known about self-hypnosis before the other two boys were born, how much easier things would have been.

It is almost impossible to assess how many hypnotic sessions will be needed by someone suffering from a phobia. So much depends on the patients themselves — whether they can cooperate, whether they do their homework, whether they feel the need to probe into the past and find out why the phobia appeared in the first place, or whether they are content just to go ahead and get rid of it.

Jenny comes to me for a regular 'top-up', as she calls it. Jenny's problems are unlikely to go away: as well as two fit and healthy children, she has to care for a young son who is severely disabled, both mentally and physically.

She was a patient of mine some five years ago when she was in a very depressed state and unable to cope. She proved to be an excellent subject, responding marvellously to treatment and working very hard on her own too, so that she improved beyond recognition in just a few weeks. She has never regressed to the distressed and distressing state she was in when first I met her, but every year or so she comes for a booster treatment which helps her to keep going.

When patients consult me for the first time, I can only estimate how often I will need to see them. However, I do always say that they should be aware of some positive progress — which does not necessarily mean a complete cure — after four visits. If not, then it may be that we are not going to succeed, and I may suggest that they should consult a different therapist. This happens only rarely, and is not necessarily the fault of either the patient or myself — there may be a lack of rapport between us, or perhaps it is not the time for that particular patient to be helped by hypnosis.

I can only speak for myself in my dealings with patients; nevertheless I suggest that when you consult a hypnotherapist, you should always find there has been a positive step forward after you have had four sessions. This does not mean that there may not be a temporary setback at some later date; but if, after four hypnotic sessions, you really do not detect any change in yourself or in your condition, then it might be wiser to change either your therapy or your therapist.

How can I find a good hypnotherapist?
As the law stands at the moment it is possible for anyone to set up as a hypnotherapist. There are, however, several honest and extremely efficient training courses, and on pages 125-6, you will find addresses you can write to for lists of therapists who have been properly trained. But remember that a therapist who does not appear on one of those lists may be equally genuine and good at his or her job.

Below are a few hints about choosing the therapist who is right for you:

1. Having selected a therapist to visit, do not be afraid to ask about training and any qualifications.

2. Reputable hypnotherapists should be willing to discuss hypnosis with you, and to answer any questions you might have. They should also be prepared to give you a taste of hypnosis by doing some sort of test on you, to show that you can be hypnotized and just what it feels like. This should be done free of charge.

3. I would feel a little doubtful about any hypnotherapist who wants to charge you for a specific number of sessions before you even begin treatment. It is not possible to say accurately just how many sessions will be needed, and I believe it is unethical to take the money for, say, eight sessions when perhaps only four are really necessary.

Therapists are certainly justified in asking you to pay in advance for your next visit, so that if you are unable to come at the last minute and they have to sit in their consulting room with nothing to do, they are recompensed for that lost session. But to charge for a 'full course', as is sometimes done, when no one can say precisely how long a 'full course' needs to be, is not the right way of doing it.

4. Lastly, and perhaps most essentially, rely on your instinct. If you take an instant dislike to the hypnotherapist, whether that dislike is justified or not, you are not going to respond in the right way and so there is no point in even starting the treatment. Whereas if you feel that you have confidence in the therapist and could get along with him or her fairly well, then that is quite a good indication that the treatment is likely to be successful.

Is hypnosis expensive?

The fee for a session of hypnotherapy naturally varies from area to area. On average you can expect to pay (1997 fees) between £20 and £50 per session depending on the area – the highest rate applying in the large cities.

Whether or not you consider this expensive depends on your priorities. How do you value, in financial terms, the overcoming of a long-term problem? What price can be put on freedom from stress? It is comparatively simple to work out the money saved by a former smoker, but more difficult to assess the financial worth of sound, untroubled sleep — yet who is to say which result is of greater benefit?

Can hypnosis be dangerous?

The short answer is 'never', at least not in the hands of a competent and ethical hypnotherapist. The worst thing that can happen to you is that nothing will happen. Because you will always hear and understand precisely what is going on, and because you have your own mind and will, you cannot be made to do anything you do not wish to do.

In addition, there is no such thing as being left in a half-hypnotized or semi-trance state — you are either under hypnosis or you are not. The only difference you should be aware of when you have finished a hypnotic session is that you are far more relaxed than you were before you started.

This does *not* mean that you will not be in full control of all your faculties and able to act and react in precisely the same way as usual.

How will I be hypnotized?

There are various techniques, and each therapist has his or her own favourite. You are unlikely to find anyone anxious to swing a watch on a chain before your eyes — and I am not too certain that I would be happy with that particular therapist if you did. The most common methods of being hypnotized include:

- staring at a hypnotic spiral disc (see page 23);
- being asked to gaze at a fixed point on the ceiling, or at a pinpoint of light, and as the therapist talks to you and leads you into the hypnotic state, finding

that your eyes need to close;
- sitting in a comfortable chair (or lying on a couch) and closing your eyes with the therapist guiding you verbally through a physical and then a mental relaxation technique, before counting you down into the hypnotic state.

I prefer to use the last method because I feel that a patient who starts off with eyes closed will concentrate far more on my voice and what I am saying, and will not be so aware of possible outside distractions.

How will I know that I am hypnotized?

This is where the hypnosis test, first mentioned on page 21, comes into its own. There are two main reasons for testing the susceptibility of a new patient to hypnosis. The first is that the hypnotic state never feels as people expect it to. Most people anticipate being completely unconscious and unaware of what the therapist is saying. When this does not, in fact, happen, there is a tendency for patients to think that the therapist has failed, and that they have not been hypnotized at all.

The idea of the test is to prove to patients that they have indeed been hypnotized. The therapist can tell it has happened by a change in the rhythm of the patients' breathing and by movement behind the eyelids, but the patients themselves will not be aware of this. It therefore becomes necessary to prove to them that they are indeed good subjects for hypnosis. I cannot, of course, tell you precisely what the test will be; there are various techniques and they all work; but if you know in advance what is going to be said and are 'waiting' for it, then it will not be as effective.

The second reason for testing new patients is that, when the therapist begins the actual treatment, they will already have experienced the feeling of being hypnotized, and so will be able to concentrate on the words they are hearing rather than wondering whether this is what hypnosis is supposed to feel like.

Will the symptoms return if I stop having treatment?

The idea behind hypnotherapy is not to create dependency, but to cure the patient. If a patient cannot survive without a regular 'dose' of hypnosis, then the therapist has not done his or her job properly.

An exception to this rule would be the case of someone like Jenny, the mother of the handicapped child, described on pages 42-3. By means of hypnotherapy, Jenny successfully overcame the depression which threatened her. She is an intelligent woman who realizes that an occasional visit will prevent this feeling of depression returning, even though there can be little change in her daily routine and responsibilities.

In other cases there may be the occasional need for a follow-up visit some time after treatment has ended. Peter came to me a while ago to ask for help in giving up smoking. He proved to be an excellent subject and stopped completely after three sessions. I heard nothing more for about two years, and then he telephoned in a panic. Apparently he had just suffered a tragedy in his personal life, and although he had not touched a cigarette for the whole of the two-year period, he had been offered one when he was feeling at his lowest ebb and had taken it and smoked it.

Despite the fact that he did not particularly enjoy it, he had had two or three more since, and he was afraid that it would not be long before he became a smoker again — something which he did not wish to happen. I asked Peter to come and see me for just one hypnotic session; in that session I was able to reinforce all his old desire to be and remain a non-smoker. He is a non-smoker to this day.

Can I be hypnotized from a distance?

We have all seen films and plays where the telephone rings and the subject answers it, only to hear some 'magic' signal or trigger word which immediately produces a zombie-like hypnotic trance. Equally, we have also all seen cowboy films where the hero, armed only with a short-range pistol, aims at a far-off target which is rapidly moving away and is able to score a perfect shot.

CAN YOU HYPNOTISE ME FROM A DISTANCE?

One scenario is as realistic as the other. The only way in which the hypnotherapist will have a far-reaching effect on you is if he or she has given you a post-hypnotic suggestion which you have heard, clearly understood and voluntarily accepted.

Can anyone learn to be a hypnotherapist?
The ability to hypnotize others can be learned by anyone of reasonable intelligence. It is an acquired skill, not a special gift enjoyed by only a privileged few. It is comparatively easy to teach someone to put others into a hypnotic state. The real test of skill, learning and expert knowledge lies in being able to help them overcome their problems once they have been hypnotized.

3.
RELAXATION AND VISUALIZATION

When I first started working as a hypnotherapist some years ago, the vast majority of my patients came to see me because they wanted to lose weight, to give up smoking or to overcome some particular fear or phobia.

But all that has changed. At least 70 per cent of those who consult me now come because they are suffering from stress, tension, anxiety, lack of confidence, depression, or what they call 'nerves'. Whatever name you give to the condition, in effect it all comes under the heading of 'stress'. It is a sad fact that in our modern world, with all its so-called advantages, people have lost the ability to relax.

RELAXATION

Relaxation is something which can easily be learned, and hypnosis is the ideal method for teaching it. Once someone has learned the art of true relaxation, it becomes a part of that person's very nature. The ability to relax is one of the most wonderful gifts you can give yourself.

No one is suggesting that being able to relax, to shut out the pressures and tensions of the everyday world, is going to put an end to the cares and problems which surround you. It will, however, put you in a sufficiently calm and clear-thinking frame of mind to be able to deal with those problems to the very best of your ability. In addition, because so many of today's illnesses are caused by an inability to cope with stress, learning to relax can have a very beneficial effect on your physical well-being.

Relaxation is quite often the first thing I teach when a patient comes to consult me — even if the problem does not appear to the patient to be stress-related. Heavy smokers will usually reach for a cigarette when they have a particularly knotty problem to handle at work, or if they have to walk into a room full of strangers. Take away the stress factor, and the smoking problem often becomes far less.

Students unable to retain the facts they are trying to learn for an important exam are often so tense and anxious about their studies that the tension itself closes the avenues of their minds and memories. More obviously, the majority of fears and phobias are caused by someone with a vivid imagination being terrified of what *might* happen and reacting to the stress of that imagined situation. So, in many cases, the first essential is to teach patients how to relax mentally and physically, and then let them go home and spend a week or so practising these techniques before proceeding with further treatment.

THE BENEFITS OF RELAXATION

Acquiring this technique of relaxation brings two important benefits. One is that, by learning to relax, you are often far more able to see and understand your own problems clearly. I have even known of one or two cases where a patient has returned to me after the initial relaxation training saying that the problem 'appears to have vanished'. All this proves, of course, is that sometimes the problem is nothing more than tension itself. The second important benefit of learning how to relax and practising it for yourself is that it will make you a far better subject for hypnosis when more specific treatment is called for.

Relaxation has wonderful side-effects, too. From the

very first time that you are taught how to relax under hypnosis, you will begin to feel the benefits. There is an increased sense of serenity, both mental and physical. This makes you far less likely to become irritable or lose your temper with those day-to-day annoyances which we all have to face. After all, if you lose your temper, you will usually end up feeling far worse than the person who caused the irritation in the first place. It will be your heart which races, your fists which clench and unclench, your temples which throb and — whether you realize it or not — your judgment which may be seriously impaired for some considerable time afterwards.

Relaxation can also work wonders physically. I cannot begin to count the number of my patients who have discovered that what they thought of as lumbago, rheumatism or just generalized 'back trouble' completely disappeared once they learned to relax — even if those problems were nothing to do with their initial reason for consulting me.

Headaches, too, can seem to vanish like magic. Unless there is some external cause, such as a bang on the head, eye strain or a specific allergy, it is technically impossible for a totally relaxed person to suffer from a headache. Even for the majority of migraine sufferers, headaches can become a thing of the past.

Right from the start, when you begin to practise true relaxation, you are likely to find that you sleep much more deeply and with less nocturnal tossing and turning. That sleep will be clearer and less troubled, and you will wake refreshed and ready to face the coming day. This in itself adds to your general feeling of being calmer and more relaxed. In this way relaxation can set in motion a therapeutic — as opposed to a vicious — circle.

How are you sitting now as you read these words? Are your shoulders tensed? Is there a frown marring your forehead? Are you clenching your teeth? Relax. Let all the tension go out of your body. Take a few deep breaths before you read any further. Let your jaw sag just a little. Uncross your legs — you would be amazed just how much physical tension is caused by the simple act of crossing your legs. Stand up, if at all possible, and literally shake the tension from your arms and legs.

I usually suggest to my patients that they try to get into the habit, every now and then throughout the day, of stopping to think about whether or not they are subjecting their bodies to unnecessary tension. Because if they are, they are also subjecting their minds to unnecessary tension. It only takes a moment of each person's time to make a conscious effort to release that tension — and it is a moment very well spent. Once you have begun through hypnosis to learn the techniques of relaxation, you will find fewer and fewer occasions when you are aware of that tension in your body. Relaxation will eventually become second nature.

Through hypnosis it is possible to develop a relaxed mental attitude as well as a relaxed physical body. You can learn to pause before reacting. Obviously there are times when this would be utterly ridiculous. If you are standing in the middle of the road and there is a huge double-decker bus hurtling towards you, naturally that is *not* the time to stop and think — that is the time for a very quick reaction indeed!

take a deep breath.
breathe out slowly,
relax shoulder
muscles....

OBVIOUSLY THERE ARE TIMES WHEN IT WOULD BE
RIDICULOUS TO PAUSE BEFORE REACTING ......

But there are many, many times during the day when petty annoyances may cause you to react quickly and sharply. Someone who has been helped to learn to relax will get into the habit of pausing briefly before reacting. During that moment you will ask yourself whether the situation is one which justifies losing your patience or feeling aggravated, especially when either of these reactions is likely to leave you in a state of tension, possibly for hours.

What is this relaxation technique which your hypnotherapist is likely to teach you? How often do you have to practise it — and when is the best time to do it? Described below is the method I use when dealing with my own patients. Although all therapists will differ slightly in their techniques, this is a very typical routine, and one which you are likely to encounter whichever therapist you consult.

LEARNING HOW TO RELAX

You will be asked to sit in a comfortable chair, or perhaps to lie on a couch. Then, having used his or her own particular induction technique to put you into a hypnotic state, the therapist will ask you to concentrate on the different areas of your body, one at a time, usually working upwards from the feet.

As you concentrate on your feet, the suggestion will be given to you that they are beginning to feel very warm and very heavy. Because you are open to suggestion and because you are allowing your mind to cooperate with the therapist, your feet will indeed begin to feel warm and heavy. You may experience a slight tingling feeling — a little like pins and needles but not in any way painful — and the whole sensation is very soothing.

Once it is obvious to the therapist that the suggestion is taking effect, he or she will begin to work very slowly upwards, asking you to concentrate on your legs and thighs, then your hands and arms, the whole of the trunk of your body, your shoulders, neck and head, ending with the suggestion that your eyelids and your jaw too are heavy and comfortable. By this stage you will often find that the therapist's voice may seem a little distant, but at no time will you lose awareness of what is going on. You will still be in full control of the situation — you are just relaxing because you want to.

Once you have achieved that state of physical relaxation, the next stage is to relax your mind. I always find that the easiest and most effective way to help new and possibly slightly nervous patients to do this is to take them on a mental walk. I like to guide this walk myself, rather than leave it to the patients to invent their own. The reason for this is that if I am dealing with people who are anxious or depressed, and I leave them to their own imaginings, they are likely to incorporate something horrific in their mental image of the walk.

By that time, however, patients will have become used to my voice and to accepting my gentle suggestions about physical relaxation, and as a result will usually be quite content to accept the images I put forward. Although these images will vary from patient to patient, they all involve a walk in pleasant surroundings of one sort or another, and emphasize the heightened awareness of the different senses — perhaps the feeling of sunshine, the sound of the sea, the song of birds, the scent of flowers — whatever I happen to feel is most suitable for that particular person.

PRACTISING AT HOME

Before I bring patients out of the hypnotic state, I tell them when and how I want them to practise both the physical and the mental elements of this technique for themselves. In most cases the ideal time for such practice is in bed at night, in the half-and-half time when you are neither awake nor asleep. Experts have proved that we are most susceptible to suggestion immediately prior to sleeping and immediately prior to waking. As it is virtually impossible to control what happens just before waking, the period just before sleep seems ideal for this exercise.

Miracles are rare indeed and no overnight change in condition is likely, but I have yet to find a patient who has practised these techniques on a regular basis who has not felt some benefit within the first week.

There is a very sound reason for giving the instructions to patients while they are still in the hypnotic state, rather than waking them first and just talking to them. Many people find that they are able to relax so well after the first few attempts that they actually fall asleep during the exercise. Provided the suggestion has been given and accepted post-hypnotically — that, is to say, while the patient was still in the hypnotic state — then the subconscious mind will allow the walk to continue, even though the conscious mind may have 'shut down' for the night and not be aware of what is happening. Your subconscious mind will not forget anything which it wishes to remember if you have been told it while hypnotized.

It is impossible to practise your relaxation technique too often. If you suffer from tension, you can derive additional benefit from extra practice during the day as well as when you go to bed at night. You will do yourself no harm — and probably quite a lot of good.

THE POWER OF THE IMAGINATION

Once you have become accustomed to using your imagination and your ability to visualize in order to relax, you can go on to use it in other ways, particularly when you find yourself in or approaching a situation which is likely to be stressful.

Most people do not realize the importance of the imagination and what it can do. The dictionary describes imagination as the 'formation of mental images', or the 'creative faculty of the mind'. But those mental images can be either positive or negative. Think of the number of people who say: 'I haven't seen a doctor for years; I'm never ill.' Why are they never ill? They presumably come into contact with the same set of germs and viruses as everyone else. It is just that they see themselves as healthy people. And because that is how they see themselves, that is how they are.

But what about those who have other people's mental images forced on them? Take the parent who says: 'Don't let little Tommy carry that plate; he's bound to drop it, he's so clumsy.' Poor little Tommy may well have dropped or broken something once, and ever afterwards was told: 'Be careful. Watch what you're doing. Don't drop it', until eventually Tommy's own imagination convinces him that he really is a clumsy person. In fact, of course, he is just a person who once broke something.

How does all this relate to you? What difference does it make to your life if Mrs Smith down the road never catches a cold, or little Tommy has become a clumsy person? The answer is that we are all Mrs Smith or little Tommy. Each of us has been influenced by the positive or negative aspects of our own imagination until we have become the person we are today, with all our faults, anxieties and phobias. But anyone who possesses an imagination strong enough to influence them negatively to such an extent, can use that same imagination to change themselves positively in whatever way they wish. When that use of imagination is combined with hypnosis and relaxation therapy, it can achieve even more.

After all, every achievement starts in the imagination. The artist standing in front of the blank canvas, the sculptor gazing at a piece of cold, hard stone — each begins by imagining what they are going to do; they have a dream. Of course dreams cannot make up for lack of practical ability. It is not enough to see in your mind the beautiful picture of a sunset you want to paint. If you have never learned to mix and apply the paint correctly, the finished picture is bound to be a disappointment. But when dealing with yourself, you are more fortunate. If there is something about you as a person that you would like to change, you already have all the techniques at your fingertips, just waiting to be used.

I'd like to do something about this uncontrollable rage..

IF THERE IS SOMETHING ABOUT YOU AS A PERSON YOU WOULD LIKE TO CHANGE, YOU ALREADY HAVE THE TECHNIQUES AT YOUR FINGERTIPS, WAITING TO BE USED.

VISUALIZATION

Let me tell you about Rebecca. She came to see me a short time ago because she was concerned about certain aspects of her work. Rebecca was a highly intelligent young woman of 28, and she had risen swiftly in a large commercial organization. She had no doubts at all about her ability to cope with her daily work, but she was troubled by a weekly meeting which she had to attend. There she was expected to report on the progress her department had made during the previous seven days. The other participants at those meetings were mostly men and they were all considerably older then her, and with far more experience.

Because she was so anxious about giving a bad impression at these meetings, Rebecca always slept badly the night before. When the moment came for her to enter the boardroom, panic would set in, so that she was never able to do justice to herself or to her capabilities. The stress and tension she was experiencing were, in fact, bringing about the very situation she feared most — that of appearing less experienced and less capable than she knew herself to be.

When she came to see me for hypnotherapy, Rebecca turned out to be an excellent subject — as highly intelligent people usually are. On the first visit, I merely taught her a relaxation technique which I asked her to practise at home before we tackled her specific anxieties.

On her second visit, I began by again talking Rebecca into the relaxed state she was now used to — and, naturally, because she had been practising this for herself, it took only a few minutes. I then gave her a post-hypnotic suggestion of the image she was to conjure up in her mind. I told her to see herself standing outside the door of the boardroom just before the start of the weekly meeting. But I emphasized that, in her imagination, she was to be aware of feeling calm and relaxed.

From then on everything was to happen exactly as it normally did, except that Rebecca was to be aware of feeling completely at ease and was to deliver her weekly report and answer any questions on it in a confident and self-assured manner — and she was to be aware, too, of the approval of her colleagues for the work she had done. Before I brought her out of the hypnotic state, I instructed Rebecca to repeat this process at least once a day until the next meeting, and to make sure she did it on the night before the meeting itself.

Actors rehearse their parts so that their performance will be perfect on the night. This was Rebecca's rehearsal. She continued to practise her relaxation and to 'rehearse' the scene in her mind every night for a week prior to the dreaded meeting. When the meeting eventually took place, it was merely a repeat of what she had been mentally rehearsing — and so it was easy. She was word perfect. The whole thing went smoothly. Rebecca gave her report in a calm, confident manner, aware all the time of a feeling of mental and physical relaxation. When her report had been given, she received the praise of her colleagues and superiors. And, of course, having done it once, Rebecca had erased the need for anxiety on future occasions.

Perhaps this sounds like magic or a fairy tale to you — but I can assure you that this particular story (apart from the name I have given you) is absolutely true. And the method can be adapted to fit any anxiety you have about yourself. The advantage of using hypnosis for a process like this is that it eliminates the self-doubt which is present in all of us. If I were to tell you now to imagine yourself as a success in your chosen sphere, you would not find it easy to do. Doubts creep in. Your conscious mind might interfere by introducing niggling little thoughts such as, 'Of course I don't believe it can really work', or 'I couldn't really do that'. But, as we have already established, hypnosis can bypass the objections of the conscious mind, and address itself specifically to the subconscious.

If you have a dream at night, that dream could be something quite ridiculous — perhaps you are in a house which sprouts wings and flies to China — anything at all. And, although you may laugh at yourself when you wake in the morning, at the time you have the dream it all seems perfectly logical. Your conscious mind is asleep, so cannot interfere to say, 'Don't be silly; that couldn't happen'.

In just the same way, when you are hypnotized, your conscious mind is so relaxed that it does not interfere when the hypnotherapist puts the suggestion of success into your mind. From then on, once you have accepted the original suggestion, it is in your subconscious mind; so in the same way that you accept a dream, you accept the possibility that you can achieve what you want.

4.
SMOKING AND OBESITY

SMOKING

The first thing I always ask prospective patients who tell me that they want to stop smoking is, 'Do you really want to give it up?' This is not as foolish as it might appear. Many people decide to give up smoking because they feel that they *should* — perhaps because it is becoming socially less acceptable, perhaps because of some vague niggling concern about how their health might suffer in the future.

Others profess a desire to stop smoking when in fact it is someone else who wants them to stop. Maybe their doctor has advised them that their health would improve — as, undoubtedly it would — if they were to avoid smoking altogether; in other cases a wife or husband may be pressuring them to stop — particularly if he or she has recently succeeded in giving up. But if the patient is really only trying to give up for someone else's sake, the therapy will not succeed. Under such circumstances I am not prepared even to start a course of treatment, since it would be a waste of my time, the patient's money — and would achieve nothing in the end.

REASONS FOR GIVING UP

If patients can assure me that they genuinely *want* to give up smoking, I then have to find out the reasons why. This is very important for the therapist, as it is these reasons (and often fears) which will be incorporated into the

treatment itself. Some of the most common reasons are
given below:

The patient's own health. As well as the obvious and
well-publicized fear of lung cancer, there is very real
reason for a smoker to be concerned about developing
bronchitis, heart disease, hardening of the arteries,
shortness of breath or susceptibility to a stroke, since all of
these are encouraged by smoking.

The health of others. The children of parents who
smoke are far more likely to smoke themselves than the
children of parents who do not. Many responsible adults
fear that, even if they themselves were to escape the many
and various health hazards which threaten a smoker, their
children might not. And no caring parent wants to be
responsible for the future suffering of their children.

It has also been proved that babies born to mothers who
smoked during pregnancy are far more likely to suffer
from some sort of deficiency, at birth or soon afterwards.
These babies often weigh less when they are born than the
babies of non-smokers. This of course makes them far
more susceptible to illness and infection in early life.
Because of these problems, many responsible women are
anxious to stop smoking before they even allow themselves
to become pregnant, so there can be no danger of
adversely affecting their unborn child.

Being 'nice to be near'. However careful about
personal freshness and cleanliness, there is no way that a
smoker can avoid the unpleasant odours which
accompany the habit. If someone smokes, then their
clothes are bound to smell — and others will be even more
aware of this fact than the actual smoker. Very few
people, once they realize it, are happy to go around with
their clothes smelling of stale tobacco smoke. Even less do
they want to think that their hair, their skin and even
their breath smells of stale smoke. Understandably, they
find it distressing to think that every time they speak to
someone, that person is going to be made unpleasantly

aware of the fact that they smoke — because of the foul smell of their breath.

Feeling fit. The person who complains of feeling less fit than previously usually finds that this awareness has crept up little by little. It's no longer possible to climb the stairs without getting breathless. Walking has become much more of an effort. That is when panic often sets in. The lack of fitness may be only partial, but the fear is that it will get worse as time goes on.

Self-esteem. For some people, smoking may epitomize the fact that they are no longer in charge of their own lives. Every time they say, 'I enjoy a cigarette after a meal' or 'I need a cigarette at times of stress' or 'I only smoke to be sociable', what they are really saying is, 'I cannot exist without tobacco. Tobacco is my master'.

TOBACCO IS MY MASTER

Terry came to me because he realized that this was what was happening to him. He suddenly felt that he did not want his life to be ruled by anything other than himself — certainly not by something as ridiculous as a handful of crushed, dried-up leaves. He decided that anything he did in the future was to be because he chose and not because he felt compelled to do it. And that is why he is going to succeed.

Finance. Surprisingly enough, this comes quite low down on the list of reasons why people say they want to give up smoking. Even those who have taken the time and trouble to work out just what sort of holiday they could have each year if only they did not smoke, rarely put this forward as a prime reason for giving up. It seems to be merely a pleasant bonus to find more money in the kitty at the end of each month than before.

WHY OTHER METHODS FAIL

Those who seek help from a hypnotherapist to give up smoking usually do so as a last resort. They have already tried every other method they can think of, and have proved to themselves that these other methods do not work. Some of the methods almost doomed to fail include:

Willpower. Willpower on its own scarcely ever made anyone give up smoking permanently — although it can help on a temporary basis. If you take time to think about it, the reason is quite obvious.

If you like to smoke, if you enjoy the taste and sensation of smoking, and then try to force yourself to stop, what are you actually doing? You are setting up an internal conflict, the same sort of conflict which arises whenever you try to make yourself do something you do not really want to do. That conflict causes more tension and more stress; and, of course, the more stress you feel, the more urgent is your need to smoke. Eventually the day will come when you can take the stress no longer, and you find yourself reaching for the comfort of a cigarette. That is why people who use willpower to give up smoking almost always fail and, with very few exceptions, will return to the habit sooner or later.

Cutting down. Cutting down on the number of
cigarettes you smoke during a day is very unlikely to help
you give up altogether. Why? There are two main reasons.
The first is a physical reason. By merely cutting down
your intake, you are not actually ridding your body of its
nicotine addiction. As the addiction remains with you, so
does the likelihood that, at any time, you may find
yourself returning to old habits.

The other reason is a psychological one. When you cut
down the amount you smoke, you tend to count the hours
— if not the minutes — between cigarettes. By doing this
you are filling your mind with thoughts of smoking —
whereas, to succeed in giving up once and for all, you
really need to spend as little time as possible thinking
about the habit.

Nicotine chewing gum. This is often prescribed by
doctors to those who want to give up smoking.
Unfortunately, like cutting down, it merely prolongs
rather than relieves the nicotine craving.

WHY HYPNOTHERAPY WORKS

Hypnotherapy is an excellent way to give up smoking. Not
only is there a very high success rate, but those who have
given up tend not to go back to the habit.

The reason is easy to understand. With hypnosis you
are not being forced to do something you do not really
want to do — no one is pressuring you or trying to exert
their will over you. All that is happening is that you are
being gently helped to do something you really want to do.
But you are being *helped* — not compelled. What you
finally achieve, you achieve for yourself.

Another advantage of using hypnosis is that smoking
itself is often very closely linked with stress. Most people
who smoke started in their teenage years. They were
insecure and wanted to appear more adult — cigarettes
gave them a false sense of self-assurance. Had those
teenagers been more confident in the first place, they

would never have needed the prop of smoking. Adults who smoke also do so mainly at times of stress. Because hypnosis begins by creating a feeling of total relaxation, it is possible at one and the same time to treat the smoking, and the nervousness which led to it.

Whatever your reason for wanting the therapy, hypnosis will enable you to know and understand yourself better as an individual. As a result it will also make you realize, should you be a smoker, that if you smoke 20 cigarettes a day, you probably do not *enjoy* more than five or six of them. Some people find that they really enjoy the cigarette they have after a meal; with others it is the first cigarette of the day — or perhaps the last one before bed. I have never yet met anyone who could honestly say that they actually enjoyed *every* cigarette they smoked. To risk your health and even your life for something which gives you great pleasure might just be understandable; but to do it for something which is no more than a habit seems foolish in the extreme.

HOW MANY VISITS WILL IT TAKE?

It is impossible to say precisely how many sessions of hypnosis will be needed by any individual.

I usually expect my patients to be non-smokers within three visits. Having said that, I have known of some patients who have stopped smoking altogether after just one session — but that is fairly unusual. There have also been cases of people who required five or even six sessions — but this too is not the norm. Three to four sessions seems to be the average.

The very fact that it is impossible to predict with any degree of accuracy how long it will take someone to become a non-smoker only serves to reinforce my belief that it is unethical for a hypnotherapist to take money in advance for a specific number of sessions — there is no point at all in making a patient pay for unnecessary treatment. Similarly, any embarrassment which might arise because an extra session or two is needed can be avoided.

You will notice how I referred above to the patient becoming a *non-smoker*. It is very important that patients learn to think of themselves as non-smokers rather than as lapsed smokers or ex-smokers. A non-smoker does not smoke; an ex-smoker can always go back to it.

WHAT FORM WILL THE TREATMENT TAKE?

Having begun by guiding you into a pleasant state of relaxation, the hypnotherapist will then use suggestion to remind your subconscious mind of all the things about smoking which you do not like. There is no point at all in hypnotizing someone and merely repeating, 'When you wake up you will not smoke', over and over again. This achieves nothing permanent at all. What the therapist has to do is to persuade your subconscious mind that you dislike smoking and all that goes with it.

Depending on what you said to the therapist before the treatment started, emphasis will be placed on the particular aspects of smoking which you personally find unpleasant. Once your subconscious mind accepts the suggestion that smoking is unpleasant, for whatever reason, it is actually very easy indeed for you to give up — and to give up permanently. After all, no one ever found difficulty in giving up something they did not like doing; we only cling to those things which we really enjoy.

If it is possible to put this dislike of smoking and everything concerned with it into the subconscious mind on the first visit, you may wonder why subsequent visits are ever necessary. The answer is that, having disposed of the craving, we still have to deal with the habit.

We have established that the average smoker will only actually enjoy a very small proportion of the cigarettes smoked in the course of a day. The remainder are consumed out of habit. Some people have an almost Pavlovian response to the sound of the telephone ringing and, as they go to answer it, they automatically reach for the cigarette packet. Others will light a cigarette immediately after a meal without stopping to consider whether or not they really want to smoke — sometimes they will hardly even realize that they *are* smoking. Because all patients are human beings with human fallibilities, should someone offer them a cigarette, they will quite often accept without even stopping to remember that they have no wish to smoke any more. Similarly, at times of stress, people may reach for the cigarette packet purely out of habit — it is something they have always done — a reflex action with little or no thought behind it.

SOME SMOKERS HAVE A PAVLOVIAN RESPONSE TO A BELL RINGING ....

So, having disposed of the actual desire to smoke, it is then necessary to spend some time curbing the habit. This will often be done by aversion therapy — that is, by persuading your subconscious mind that the cigarette taken without thought will taste unpleasant. This unpleasant taste serves to remind you that you are now a non-smoker and should put the cigarette out immediately.

As I have said, only those who really want to give up smoking can be helped by hypnosis; and, because of this fact, it is my policy never to accept patients who cannot honestly tell me that this is what they want. On one occasion only did I make an exception to this rule. I was approached by a local doctor who told me about one of his patients, a man of 42, who had so damaged his health by very heavy smoking that he had already undergone open-heart surgery. This man (I will call him John) had been told by the specialist that unless he stopped smoking altogether, he was unlikely to live for more than a few months. The doctor asked me if I would accept John as a patient and try to help him.

When I spoke to John, he told me that he could not bear the thought of giving up smoking. Nevertheless, against my better judgment, I said that I would see if I could help him through hypnosis. After four sessions John was still smoking as heavily as ever and showed no desire even to cut down the number of cigarettes he smoked each day. Four months later he died.

It still seems incredible to me that a man of only 42 could prefer smoking to living, but this was actually so. This rather sad case only goes to prove that you, the patient, are always the one in control, and that with hypnosis you will not be made to do anything you do not wish to do.

BEFORE TREATMENT STARTS	AFTER THE FIRST SESSION	AFTER THE SECOND SESSION	AFTER THE THIRD SESSION
Stress Desire Habit Addiction	Desire Habit Addiction	Habit Addiction	Addiction (fades with time)

The stages of giving up smoking

OBESITY

To become aware of the extent of the obesity problem in the West at the present time, one only has to take note of the vast numbers of organizations, books, clubs and so-called 'miracle diets' which abound — most of which make considerable sums of money for their creators. The problem, however, is very much more complex than is generally realized. As well as those who grow fat as a result of overeating, there are those who have

69

some medical condition such as an underactive thyroid gland (although this group is fairly small). But by far the greatest number of obese people are overweight because of some deep emotional problem.

Looking at these groups one by one, we can assess whether and to what extent they can be helped by hypnotherapy.

Those with a medical problem causing overweight:

If someone is suffering from obesity because of a genuine glandular or other physical malfunction, then hypnotherapy is not the answer. But the proportion of overweight people to whom this applies is very small indeed, compared to the number of people who are only too willing to blame their excess weight on it. If a physical malfunction is the cause of excess weight, then medical help, whether traditional or alternative, is required and should be sought.

Those who eat too much because of appetite:

There is a large group of people who have become accustomed to eating too much because of early programming or through habit. Such people need to learn to listen to their appetite, and to control their eating on a more practical and deliberate level. Within this group you will find people who have grown up to expect healthily (or rather, unhealthily) large portions of food on their plates at mealtimes — and to finish every morsel of it. In that group, too, are the business people accustomed to heavy lunches with their clients.

We are all victims of food programming in one way or another. Who has not heard adults say, 'Have you hurt yourself? Don't cry — have cake with your tea'; or 'You've been such a good girl today — here's some chocolate for you'. These often well-intentioned remarks have been the cause of many a weight problem in later life.

'Eat everything on your plate or you won't grow up a big strong boy'; 'There are starving children all over the world

AS CHILDREN WE HAVE LITTLE OR NO CHOICE AS TO HOW MUCH OR HOW LITTLE WE EAT.

who would be only too grateful for what's on your plate'; 'If you don't finish your lunch you won't have any sweets afterwards'. Those whose weight problem has been caused by this kind of programming can be helped quite quickly and effectively by hypnosis. What they have to do is to learn to be more aware, and to listen to their subconscious minds and to their bodies.

Look at the animal kingdom and you will realize that the only overweight animals are the ones fed by humans. It is not unusual for an animal in the wild to stop eating when it feels it has had enough, even when there is still food left. That creature has learned to listen to its needs.

In your brain you have your own *appestat* — a centre that controls the appetite. The overeating problem arises because of the time lapse between your actually eating food and the registering of this fact in your brain. If you continue to eat during this interim period, by the time your brain has registered that you have had enough, you may well have consumed yet another round of sandwiches or another piece of cake.

When we are children, we do not usually have the chance to listen to the appetite control centre in our brains. We have little or no choice as to how much or how little we eat. It is usually the mother who puts a certain amount of food on the plate, and the mother who insists that children should 'be good and finish it all up'. Like any other of our senses when not used, the *appestat* becomes dulled.

Through hypnosis it is possible to learn to become aware of it again.

Those who overeat because of emotional problems:

To a certain extent this type of overeating is also caused by programming. Consider the tiny baby who cries because he is hungry. His mother feeds him, makes a fuss of him, cuddles him. The hunger disappears and the attention is pleasurable, so the baby stops crying.

But babies are clever. They soon learn that if they cry they will not only get food, but all that lovely loving. The mother, however, is not always quite so clever. She hears the baby crying and thinks, 'Poor little thing; he must be hungry'; so, as well as giving the baby the affection he wants, she gives him food — which he may not actually have wanted but which he will quite willingly accept. It does not take long for food to become linked in his mind with love and caring. Then you have the beginning of a problem.

Many people overeat for emotional reasons. Some eat because, as a result of the care they received as a baby, eating for them equals love. And, particularly if there is no love in their life at the time, obsessive eating gradually takes over. Others use their excess weight as an excuse, or as a shield behind which they can hide.

When Sally came to see me, she had been married to Phil for seven years. The marriage was not a particularly successful one; although Phil was not unkind to his young wife, he was more concerned with his career and tended to neglect her. Two years earlier Sally had had a brief affair with the husband of a friend. The affair had been shortlived and neither of them had mentioned it to their respective spouses. Since that time Sally's weight had soared. She would go on eating binges where literally she would sit and eat anything and everything for days at a time.

By the time she came to see me, Sally really felt that she hated herself. She hated her looks and her lack of control over her eating habits. What Sally failed to realize was that she was in fact so overwhelmed by guilt over that earlier affair, that she had been working away at a subconscious level to make herself as unattractive as possible so the temptation would not arise again. Initially, I did not treat her for a weight problem, but rather for lack of self-confidence and to rid herself of the guilt she had 'carried around' for two years. Once she had overcome that, it was a comparatively simple matter for her to lose weight, and required very little in the way of treatment from me.

The Baby

Feels hunger ⟶ Cries	⟶	Given food and comfort
Wants comfort ⟶ Cries	⟶	Given food and comfort

The Child

Unhappy	⟶	Given food as a comfort
Well-behaved	⟶	Given food as a reward
Naughty	⟶	Food withheld as a punishment

The Adult

Unhappy	⟶	Eats for comfort
Guilty	⟶	Eats to punish self
Lonely	⟶	Eats because of low self-esteem

TREATING OBESITY

Treating those who are overweight through habit:

When you are treated for obesity by hypnotherapy, there is no need for a diet sheet.(There are very few overweight people who do not know the contents of every diet sheet

SOME PEOPLE EAT BECAUSE THEY FEEL GUILTY
AND WISH TO PUNISH THEMSELVES

backwards, forwards and inside out — but that seldom helps them.) With hypnotherapy you will be treated so that you learn to listen once again to your own appetite control centre.

What usually happens is that the hypnotherapist will put you in a light hypnotic state and then suggest to your subconscious mind that you have a pleasantly full feeling, rather as if you had just eaten a good and satisfying meal. You will not feel bloated and uncomfortable, just satisfied. You will be told that only when it is necessary to eat for your health's sake will that full feeling disappear. Your ever-protective subconscious mind will make sure that you do not suffer in any way. What I do then is to give my patients, while they are still under hypnosis, three rules to which they must adhere.

1. Do not weigh yourself at home. There is a very simple physiological and psychological reason for this. Because of the fluctuation of the fluid in the body — particularly in the case of women — it is quite possible to obtain a false reading if you weigh yourself daily. If, for example, you were to eat more than you should on one particular day but, because of a natural adjustment of the fluid in your body, no weight gain was registered on the scales, you might begin to think

that it was quite all right to 'cheat' a little as you would
not put on weight anyway.

Similarly, should you make real progress for two days
and yet, either because of the time of the month or for
some other reason, the amount of fluid in your body
increased at that particular time, you could show a gain
in weight, giving you the impression that all your efforts
were in vain. Many a weight loss programme has been
given up in despair for just such a reason. So I insist
that my patients are weighed only by me when they
come to visit me, and that they do not jump on to the
scales between visits.

2. If you are hungry, eat. You will have been
hypnotized and told that you will only be hungry when
your body needs to have food. For the sake of your
health, therefore, when you feel actual hunger — and
that is not the same thing as having a desire for food —
you must have something to eat.

When you are being treated in this way, there is no
such thing as forbidden food. If you were told that you
could eat anything you liked with the exception of
peanuts, the first thing your subconscious mind would
want in order not to feel deprived would be peanuts. If
no food is forbidden, however, you will not get such
cravings. Obviously, common sense dictates that if you
are eating far less than usual — and that is what you
will be doing — it is better to concentrate on those foods
which are good for you; nonetheless, there is nothing
which you are actually forbidden to eat.

So, when you are hungry, you must eat. There is no
point in joining the throngs of dieters who
masochistically enjoy the hunger pangs and the
rumbling stomach — it seems to give them the
impression that they are actually achieving something
— only to rush to the cupboard when they can stand it
no longer and eat the first available food they can lay
their hands on. Since that food is usually cake or
biscuits, and since they will by then be so hungry that
they will not feel in the least inclined to wait while they

cook something nourishing, they will actually make their problem worse rather than better.

3. If you are not hungry, do not eat. How many times do you 'eat by the clock'? One o'clock — it must be lunch time; four o'clock — time for tea; six o'clock — time to prepare a meal for the evening. Such routine thinking must be put aside during treatment. It does not matter where the hands of the clock point; if you are not hungry, you must not eat anything at all.

On normal weight-loss diets, or when using one of the so-called 'magic formula' diets, a sense of deprivation builds up. A meal has to be avoided altogether — even when time and trouble has been spent preparing it. By not eating when you are not hungry, however, you are not actually being deprived of anything at all. The meal itself is not forbidden; it just has to be put to one side until you feel hungry. But it is yours; no one is saying that you cannot have it.

WHEN USING ONE OF THE SO-CALLED 'MAGIC FORMULA DIETS' A SENSE OF DEPRIVATION BUILDS UP...

When the time comes and you actually feel hungry, put half the normal amount of food on a plate and eat that. Then wait for 15 minutes. This will give your own personal *appestat* time to work, and to register the fact that food has been eaten. Once the 15 minutes have elapsed, if you can honestly say that you are still hungry, then go ahead and eat the rest of the food. But if you are no longer hungry, then do not eat any more.

If you are one of those people who has simply got into the habit of eating more than is necessary, these three rules, coupled with the hypnotic suggestion of feeling pleasantly full except when the body actually needs food, are all that is needed to ensure a weight loss. The way the method works is easy to understand; if you feel full, there is no hunger; if there is no hunger, you may not eat; if you do not eat, weight loss will ensue, whatever your personal metabolic rate.

Treating those who are overweight because of emotional problems:
The third category of overweight people is the largest. It embraces all those whose problem actually goes far deeper than a faulty *appestat* or a liking for too much food. These are the people who eat because of a deep (and deeply hidden) emotional cause.

In the case of such patients, there is no point at all in merely treating the weight problem; that will only result in the substitution of some other compensatory craving. Instead we have to begin by dealing with the emotional problem itself, forgetting temporarily about the excess weight. Quite often, if the root cause of the emotional upset can be diagnosed, the extra weight will disappear of its own accord. Once the patient has come to terms with the basic problem, it is not unusual to find that weight is lost quickly and easily without any specific treatment being needed.

The first task, therefore, is to discover why the patient eats too much. In general this can usually be attributed to a lack of confidence of one sort or another. Sometimes the patient feels unloved or unlovable — a woman who has been deserted by her husband, perhaps, who needs to find a reason for this. By making herself fat and, in her own mind, unattractive, she has an excuse to offer. 'He left me because I look so dreadful — I'm so fat', is often much easier to bear than, 'He left me because he doesn't love me any more', or 'He left me because he found someone he prefers to be with'.

Sometimes it is a more general problem of shyness or feelings of inadequacy, where the extra weight is a shield for the patient to hide behind. It provides an excuse not to join in and enjoy life, but to hide in the background.

These forms of self-dislike are often intensified by eating binges. The would-be dieter alone at home will give in to a moment's weakness and indulge in a chocolate bar. Instead of saying, 'That was silly of me. Now it might take a day or two longer to reach my desired weight', the patient is quite likely to state: 'Now I've ruined my diet. I'm a failure at losing weight, just as I am a failure at everything in life. I can't even survive for a short time without having some chocolate. I'll never succeed in losing weight — I might just as well give up altogether. I'm not worth the effort.' This may be followed by a spell of eating inordinate amounts of the wrong foods — perhaps a whole bag of doughnuts or a whole box of chocolates.

Most of the patients who come to see me with a weight problem are women. That does not mean that there are no overweight men (you only have to look around to see that isn't the case), but I have found that most men only seem to do something about their excess weight when it is linked to a health problem. Then, quite often because they have been frightened by a warning from their doctor, they are fairly successful at losing weight for themselves.

Some male patients have come to me for help in losing weight, but these usually fall into the category of those programmed to eat too much, or who have become accustomed to expense-account lunches, rather than those with a deep-seated emotional problem. That is not to say that such men do not exist, just that they seem less likely to seek help.

So, whether you are someone who has forgotten how to listen to your own appetite control register or whether there is a far deeper emotional cause for your overeating, you can be treated quite successfully by hypnosis — although completely different techniques may be used.

5.
PHOBIAS

WHAT IS A PHOBIA?

The dictionary describes a phobia as 'an irrational fear, aversion or hatred'. The important word in this context is 'irrational'. Fear in itself is not necessarily a bad thing. It is fear which prevents the Sunday stroller from attempting to climb a mountain; it is fear which sees to it that we close our front door when we leave the house; it is fear which stops you from putting your hand in the fire. These are fears of the possible or probable. They exist to protect us.

When someone has a fear of something which is only remotely possible or extremely unlikely, or a fear of something which has no basis in reality, then we are dealing with a phobia. Fears are logical and sensible; they help us to avoid doing foolish or harmful things. Phobias only serve to cause distress and unhappiness to the sufferer.

To be frightened of a huge grizzly bear is logical; to be frightened of a beetle is not. But to those who suffer from a phobia, the fear which they feel is very real indeed, and is almost impossible to overcome by strength of will alone.

Many phobias have their beginnings in the distant mists of childhood. Unthinking words, long since forgotten, can cause much emotional pain and suffering in later life.

There are over 300 listed phobias — and many more exist. Some of the most common include:

Fear	Name of phobia	Fear	Name of phobia
Bees	Apiphobia	Heights	Acrophobia
Being alone	Monophobia	Horses	Hippophobia
Being buried		Illness	Nosophobia
alive	Taphophobia	Insects	Entmophobia
Being stared		Lightning	Astropophobia
at	Scopophobia	Mice	Musophobia
Birds	Ornithophobia	Mirrors	Eisoptrophobia
Blood	Hematophobia	Needles	Belonophobia
Cats	Ailurophobia	Night	Nyctophobia
Children	Pediophobia	Open	
Choking	Pnigophobia	spaces	Agoraphobia
Crowds	Ochlophobia	Pregnancy	Maieusiophobia
Darkness	Achluophobia	Rain	Ombrophobia
Death	Necrophobia	Reptiles	Batrachophobia
Dirt	Mysophobia	School	Scholionophobia
Dogs	Cynophobia	Sea	Thalassohphobia
Dolls	Pediophobia	Sleep	Hypnophobia
Electricity	Electrophobia	Snakes	Ophidiophobia
Enclosed		Snow	Chionophobia
spaces	Claustrophobia	Solitude	Eremophobia
Feathers	Pteronophobia	Spiders	Arachnophobia
Flowers	Anthophobia	Strangers	Xenophobia
Flying	Aerophobia	Trees	Dendrophobia
Fog	Homichlophobia	Water	Hydrophobia
Germs	Spermophobia	Women	Gynophobia

TREATING A PHOBIA

These are two main methods of treating a phobia:
- regressing the patient to find out the cause of the problem and then proceeding with treatment;
- accepting that the problem exists and that the

patient wants to overcome it, and proceeding from
that point.

I will always do what patients want. If they
consider it important to discover the origins of their
phobia, I will willingly regress them to earlier periods in
their life to see whether we can uncover the cause. If they
already have some sort of idea when or how the phobia
started, that is not too difficult a task.

For example, Rosemary knew that her claustrophobia
had started at around the time of her grandmother's
death, when she was just nine years old. A little gentle
questioning under hypnosis, while Rosemary was being
regressed to the relevant age, revealed a link in the child's
mind — a link which the adult had by now forgotten —
with thoughts of being in a confined space and with her
grandmother being buried in her coffin.

Similarly, Steve knew that he had been frightened of
birds since about the age of twelve, because he could
remember that they had held no fear for him before that
time. He could not consciously remember a reason for the
fear growing, however, but over the years it had built itself
up to such a pitch that, by the time he came to see me, he
was not even able to walk past a sparrow in the street.
When he was regressed to the age of twelve, he talked of a
visit to an uncle's farm when a goose had rushed at him,
wings outstretched, and in a panic he had fallen and cut
his leg quite badly on some barbed wire. The bird had not
actually caught up with him and certainly had not
harmed him in any way, but somewhere in his
subconscious mind was the definite link between fear,
pain and birds; this had developed over the years into a
phobia which he found highly embarrassing.

In many instances, however, the patient is unable to
remember when the phobia began — it was just 'always
there'. In such cases, if patients are adamant that they
need to know the original cause, I will do my best to help
them discover it; however, it is often just as useful to say:
'You are an intelligent adult; you know that — for
whatever reason — you have this particular phobia; you

" IN HIS SUBCONSCIOUS MIND WAS THE DEFINITE LINK BETWEEN
FEAR, PAIN + BIRDS AND THIS BECAME A PHOBIA WHICH HE
FOUND HIGHLY EMBARRASSING ... "

know that you want to overcome it. Between the two of us
we can achieve this, even if we do not know the cause.'

There used to be a school of thought which said that if
one simply removed the phobia without first discovering
the cause, then another irrational fear would take its
place. But, in all the years I have been working as a
hypnotherapist, I have never once found this to be so. In
fact the reverse is often true; if one persists in probing and
prying to discover the root cause of a particular phobia,
the ever-protective subconscious will not allow the patient
to remember what must have been a traumatic
experience; or, if remembered, it will cause distress. After
all, if an experience was deep enough to create a phobia in
the first place, it may be deep enough to cause
considerable emotional pain when recalled.

Hypnosis, with its feelings of peace and relaxation, is of
course the ideal method to use when dealing with
irrational fears and phobias. From the very first visit,
patients are taught deep relaxation. Although this does

nothing for the specific problem, it is a help in their everyday life. Any sufferers from a phobia are, by definition, tense and anxious; they never know when they are going to be put in a position where their phobia will prevent them from coping. Steve, for example, with his irrational fear of birds, would find even a trip to the local shops a terrifying experience, as he never knew when he would encounter a bird in his path. For a phobic, normal life can be a nightmare.

With hypnotherapy it is possible very gently to introduce into the mind of the patient, one stage at a time, the thing which is most feared. It is important to stress here, however, that at no time should the patient be asked to do anything he or she does not wish to do. It is of no help at all for the therapist to confront the patient with a ladybird, if this is the particular phobia, or to stand an agoraphobic in an open field. This will only serve to increase rather than decrease the phobia (although at one time it was felt that this form of mental torture — for such it is — would be an instant cure). But those beliefs, along with the claim that a depressive should be told to 'snap out of it', are thankfully fast disappearing.

Hypnosis can achieve what logic cannot. When Vera first consulted me, it was for help in overcoming an absolute terror of beetles. Now I could have sat opposite Vera, without hypnotizing her, and said: 'Now Vera, you know that a beetle is a tiny little creature compared with you. It cannot sting you, bite you or hurt you in any way. You can move away, flick it away with a newspaper or even, should you feel so inclined, stamp on it. There is no logical reason for you to be afraid of it.' And Vera, unhypnotized, would have said to me: 'Yes, I understand all that you have said. I know that I have no reason to be afraid of a beetle. But the fact remains that I am terrified.'

Repeating those same logical words when Vera was in a hypnotic trance produced a very different effect. We have already seen how being in a light hypnotic trance is a bit like having a dream. Logic does not always play a part in what is going through the mind. The part of Vera's mind which would have argued with the logic presented to her was, in fact, 'asleep' when she was hypnotized, and although she was conscious of every word I said to her, she did not feel inclined to argue in her mind with what I was saying. After all, I was merely trying to help her achieve what she most wanted. She accepted the logic of the suggestion, and her phobia was overcome.

Let me tell you about Edna. Edna was an agoraphobic and had been so for the past 11 years. So bad was her condition that I had to visit her in her home; there was simply no way that she could have made the journey to see me. She could not remember how or why the fear of being outside in open spaces had begun. She just knew that month by month, year by year, it had become progressively worse — so that, by the time we met, she had literally not been outside her front door for some four years. Edna told me that she had no real desire to know why the phobia had started in the first place — she simply wanted to overcome it since, as an agoraphobic, she had almost no normal life at all.

Once I had hypnotized Edna and given her deep relaxation therapy under hypnosis, I asked her while she was still in the hypnotic state to imagine that she was standing at her own front door, with that door wide open so she could see the outside world. She did not, even in her imagination, have to set foot outside that door; she just had to look out at the front garden and the street beyond. As I spoke, I kept reminding her that she was actually in my consulting room and that she was warm, safe and comfortable. Once she had spent some minutes visualizing the scene from her front door, I gave her the post-hypnotic suggestion that she would go through this whole process each night when she was in bed, and suggested that when — but only when — she felt ready, she would actually open her front door and stand by it.

Because at all times emphasis was being placed on the feeling of calmness and relaxation, Edna did not register any signs of panic whatsoever. This told me that she would quite comfortably carry out the nightly routine in her imagination. Such a routine is designed to confuse the subconscious mind. The mind is aware that the subject is, in fact, safely tucked up in bed and out of harm's way. Because of this, even when it sees the view from the front door, it will not send out messages to the body telling the heart to race, the palms to sweat, the knees to shake — all symptoms normally felt by an agoraphobic when asked to gaze out into the open.

.. SYMPTOMS NORMALLY FELT BY AN AGORAPHOBIC WHEN SEEING THE VIEW FROM THE FRONT DOOR ..

By the time Edna actually felt able to stand at the front door with that door open, the mind had become so used to her doing it in her imagination that it 'forgot' to send out the usual panic signals. In Edna's case it took some 11 days from our first meeting to the moment when she was actually able to stand at her own open door and look out into the world beyond. This may seem a long time to learn to stand at one's own front door, but you must remember that an agoraphobic cannot normally do it without suffering all the symptoms of panic described above, as well as a number of others.

From that point on we progressed by stages — on each occasion taking the amount of time that Edna felt was necessary. The next stage was for her to imagine that she was taking three steps down her garden path, then turning and retracing those steps. When this had been accomplished, she had to walk to the front gate — and so on. After seven visits, covering some 12 weeks in time, Edna was able to lead a completely normal life. She even started driving lessons, at the age of 52.

As well as dealing with irrational fears like those of the agoraphobic, who quite often does not know what there is to be afraid of in the outside world, there are those fears which are logical in themselves but are taken to illogical lengths.

Edward was terrified by the thought of flying. There is, of course, a basis of logic in such a fear. Most people, if they are honest, have a few qualms when going in an aeroplane. They wonder about the possibility of a crash — or even these days about hijacks. Some people fortify themselves with a stiff drink to calm their nerves.

It is quite understandable why such apprehension should be at the back of any passenger's mind. Normally, however, it is counteracted by logical thoughts about there being, for example, 'more accidents on the road than in the air'. But in Edward's case, this fear had developed into a phobia of such proportions that, not only was he terrified of flying itself, but he was sent into a state of panic merely by the sound of an aeroplane flying overhead.

In such cases the hypnotherapist will appeal to the patient's logic while that patient is in the hypnotic state.

Edward having been relaxed, he was told that there was indeed a vague possibility that one day he could be in a plane which might crash, but that this possibility was so remote that it need not worry him — particularly as he was a 'holiday passenger' rather than someone who spent the major part of his life travelling on aeroplanes.

Because he was in a relaxed state, with the argumentative part of his mind safely at rest, Edward was able to accept the truth of these words. This was then combined with telling him to imagine the whole of an aeroplane journey while at the same time feeling comfortable and relaxed. It was not long before Edward overcame his fear of flying.

It is important to reassure phobia sufferers about two things. One is that they are by no means alone and that their phobia is not unusual or common just to them; the other is that there is no need to feel guilty, foolish or inadequate for having such fears. A phobia is an illness just like any other, except that the suffering tends to continue for far longer than necessary, often because phobics themselves try to disguise what they are feeling. Hypnotherapy may not be the only way of curing phobias, but it has a highly successful track record.

THE PHOBIC USUALLY TRIES TO DISGUISE WHAT HE IS FEELING ..

6.
SOME COMMON USES OF HYPNOSIS

DEPRESSION

There is a great deal of difference between what most people consider depression and the much rarer condition known as clinical depression.

Everyone has problems and worries in their lives. Sometimes, when these seem to loom large, the anxious worrier may feel 'depressed', 'down' or 'under the weather' — whatever term you wish to use. This feeling is in itself a form of illness, and benefits greatly from help and treatment.

Clincial depression, however, is far more serious, and outside help is then essential, not only from hypnotherapy but also from psychotherapy or medication given by a medical or alternative practitioner. Although hypnotherapy can greatly help those suffering from clinical depression, it is usually advisable for the patient to receive other help as well. Unfortunately, harassed doctors sometimes hand out prescriptions for pills and tablets which do nothing more than hide the symptoms of the depression, and which may cause further problems of their own, especially when the patient later attempts to stop taking the pills and suffers the side-effects which can be many and unpleasant.

But there are recognized herbal remedies which are non-addictive, and these can have a light, tranquillizing effect while doing no harm whatsoever. I am very much in favour of such remedies being used, under expert supervision, to assist the depressive patient while receiving hypnotic treatment to cope with daily life and overcome the depression itself.

A common problem I face is having to help people to withdraw gradually from the sedatives and tranquillizers which their doctors have prescribed for them. Many of these tranquillizers actually cease to have any beneficial effect at all after quite a short time, but by then the patient is usually 'hooked' and cannot stop taking the pills. Certain of them also have the effect of making the patient feel giddy when waking in the morning, and suffer pangs of nausea during the day. One of my current patients went to the doctor complaining of such symptoms, and was actually given an increased dose of the drug to help alleviate them!

But, of course, not all doctors are like that; most are deeply concerned about the drugs they prescribe for their patients, and would not dream of handing out a prescription without taking the time to note the effect of the current dosage. Only a few doctors do not see the patient on a regular basis but merely hand out repeat prescriptions on demand.

When Millie first came to see me, she was already taking six high-dose tranquillizing tablets each day. These enabled her to cope with her daily life, but only because she was in such a zombie-like state that she was hardly aware of what was going on around her. One typical incident spurred her to come and see me. She had been on a train on her way to visit an aunt in the north of England. When the train drew into the station, she was in such a state of stupor that she did not notice that she had, in fact, opened the door on the wrong side of the carriage, and she fell out onto the railway track. Fortunately for Millie, there was no train coming in the other direction. Equally fortunately, although she suffered several cuts and bruises, she was not seriously hurt. The effect of the shock, however, was to make her realize that she had to do something to overcome her dependence on tranquillizers.

When I first met Millie, about a fortnight after her experience on the train, she was trembling like a leaf — not as a direct result of the drugs, but out of fear of what would happen to her if she tried to withdraw from them. Apparently she had already made the attempt once; but, not knowing what she was doing, she had tried to stop completely rather than just cut down. The ill effects she had suffered had been so traumatic that she had never dared to try again.

I assured Millie that although in time it would be possible to reduce the number of pills considerably, and eventually perhaps do away altogether with her need for them, she certainly should not now do anything as drastic as stop taking the full dose. Our first session together was spent mostly talking, discussing the problems which had caused her to take the tranquillizers in the first place, and giving her time to build up her trust in hypnotherapy in general and in me in particular. As a depressive, she had lost all faith and trust in herself, so it was essential that she should feel she could rely on me.

I then hypnotized Millie and took her through a deep relaxation therapy, giving her the post-hypnotic suggestion which would enable her to practise this technique satisfactorily for herself at home. Relaxation, of course, was not going to solve any of Millie's external problems, but it would help her to feel stronger and more able to cope. I told her that if, after practising the technique for some days, she felt able to cut down on her present dose by one half tablet a day, she should do so — but I also

HYPNOTISM CAN HELP OVERCOME DEPENDENCE ON PILLS

reassured her that she would not have to do this unless and until she felt entirely ready to try.

I saw Millie again a fortnight later. She told me that after about five days, she had been able to take half a tablet less each day. Although she had had one or two moments of panic about it during the first couple of days, she was, in fact, now quite happy to be managing on the slightly reduced dose. We proceeded in this fashion until Millie had cut her dose by 50 per cent, before we made any attempt to deal with the underlying problems which had prompted her to seek help from her doctor in the first place.

Millie explained to me that, some time previously, her husband had left her with two young children to cope with. For the first month or two, he had not sent her any money or helped her in any way whatsoever. It was then that she had started taking tranquillizers. But that had been nearly two years ago. Since then Millie and her husband had been divorced. There had been a court order concerning maintenance which her ex-husband complied with, and the two children were now at school all day. In other words, had Millie not been taking the prescribed tranquillizers and become addicted to them, she would probably by this time have been coping with her life perfectly normally.

We continued working until Millie was able to stop taking the drugs altogether. At the same time we used hypnotherapy to help build up her general confidence again. By the end of the treatment, she was looking for a part-time job to get her, as she put it, 'back into the land of the living'.

It is important, when dealing with people addicted to drugs of any sort, to reassure them as they cut down their dose that it is *they* who are in fact achieving the desired end. The therapist can only help to point the way; without the patient's cooperation, all the therapist's efforts are of no avail. Any improvements are achieved by the commitment and hard work of the patients themselves. It is this realization which brings patients back to being able to live a full and normal life again. If they felt that it was their therapist who had 'made' them stop taking the drug, they might possibly become as addicted to the therapy as they had once been to the drug.

LACK OF CONFIDENCE

A very common thing for a new patient to say is, 'I want to be more confident'. What does that really mean? What is confidence? It would be quite possible, as was done at one time, to hypnotize the patient and say: 'Every day and in every way you are growing more confident'; and to a certain extent that kind of affirmation does serve a purpose. But on its own it will achieve little. It is only when the whole subject of confidence is broken down into the different areas of life that it is possible to set to work to improve a given situation.

'I want to become more confident' might mean 'I would like to be less shy when meeting new people'; 'I would like not to go to pieces when taking an examination'; or even 'I would like to be able to put my own views clearly in a discussion without worrying about what other people will think'. To gain confidence, it is absolutely essential to isolate the particular areas concerned. Without that, there can be no success. Having chosen one area — and, of course, there may be many — in which the patient would like greater confidence, it is possible to deal specifically with the problems which arise in that area of life.

Suppose you had taken your driving test three times and failed it on each occasion — not because of your lack of driving skill, but because your nerves always let you down. You decide to consult a hypnotherapist; what can you expect?

After the initial discussion, you will be put into a light hypnotic trance and given the necessary suggestions to make you feel secure and relaxed. Then you will be asked to allow various pictures to come into your mind, while still being aware of that feeling of relaxation and ease. The therapist will probably ask you to imagine the following scene — and at each stage remind you of how relaxed you feel, so that you are not aware of any feelings of anxiety or panic.

1. You walk into the test centre.
2. You emerge from the test centre with the examiner and walk towards the car.
3. You sit in the car and make the necessary adjustments before commencing the test.
4. During the course of the test you go through all the different techniques you have been taught to show your skills, and at each stage come through with flying colours.
5. You stop the car and turn to face the examiner who asks you questions about the Highway Code.
6. The examiner hands you a piece of paper which tells you you have passed the test.

If you were asked to picture any of these events under normal conditions, they would actually programme you for a real attack of nerves on the day itself. If, however, you picture them while at the same time being constantly reminded that you are completely relaxed and free from anxiety, then, when the time comes to take the test, you will have become a person who can actually face that situation without feeling any great nervousness.

Naturally, no amount of confidence will enable you to pass your driving test if you are unable to complete a three-point turn without hitting the kerb! But never again will you let yourself down because of your own extreme nervousness. Then the driving test will be what it was designed to be — a true test of your driving skills and ability, rather than a test of your strength of nerves.

Confidence development and positive assertion building form an integral part of any hypnotic session. They are not intended to give patients an inflated sense of their own importance, but to help them to discover their real selves. After all, no baby was ever born lacking in self-confidence. People usually lack self-confidence only as a result of their own experience or because their confidence has been destroyed by others. Sometimes this destruction may have been deliberate and malicious, but in most cases it was caused by mere thoughtlessness on the part of well-intentioned but foolish people. Many over-protective parents so smother their developing children that they are completely unable, when adult, to stand on their own two feet.

Hypnotherapy can help greatly with positive assertion training — with learning to like yourself as you really are. By means of self-hypnosis, patients are able to continue the treatment for themselves at home, and as a result their growing confidence is enhanced still further by the knowledge that they have played an active part in their own improvement.

It is often the most sensitive and creative people who are plagued by doubts about their own ability and their own worth. Goethe, Rudyard Kipling, Edgar Allen Poe, Richard Wagner and Rachmaninov — each of these highly talented men was at some point in his life the victim of depression or of insufficient self-confidence, and each of them was helped in his recovery by hypnotherapy. So, as you can see, it is by no means only the inadequates of this world who have no belief in themselves, but men and women of real brilliance too.

INSOMNIA

At one time it was believed that the hypnotic state was similar to sleep; as we saw earlier, the word 'hypnosis' comes from *hypnos* — the Greek word for sleep. Hypnosis and sleep are, in fact, not the same at all, but hypnosis is nonetheless very beneficial when dealing with insomnia.

There are several reasons why people have difficulty in sleeping well. There are, for example, those who are simply unable to let go of the problems of the day. They spend half the night worrying about all that has happened during the day which has just ended, and the other half worrying about the day which is yet to come. Many claim that they 'try' very hard to go to sleep but cannot do so.

Hypnosis treats the problem the other way around. No one ever went to sleep by 'trying'. One has to lie quietly and let sleep approach when it will. Because hypnosis enables people to relax mentally and physically, they will be in the right state of mind to receive sleep when it comes. In fact, many of my patients claim that they never actually reach the end of the relaxation exercise in bed at night — they fall asleep before they get there!

Others do actually sleep the whole night through but still feel tired and unrested when they wake. That is because they sleep so lightly that their subconscious minds are not able to dismiss their problems — whether past or present. In such cases it is often necessary to deal first with the way they are coping with the stress of their problems, so that they can achieve sufficient peace of mind to receive the full benefit from their sleep period.

Some people, for reasons which may or may not be remembered, have grown to associate sleep with death. I have found this to be the case particularly with patients who, when children, were made to look at the face of a deceased loved one, when the person looked just as if he or she were sleeping. The incident may have been long forgotten, but nonetheless it will have played its part in the child's future insomnia. Sleep becomes permanently and destructively associated with death in the subconscious mind, until there is an almost paranoic fear of allowing oneself to sleep, lest the morning never comes.

Finally, of course, there is the programming to which so many people fall victim. For some unknown reason, patients may have had difficulty in sleeping for a couple of nights — perhaps they were starting a head cold or the bedroom was too warm — and consequently they experienced tiredness the following day. The next night, when going to bed, they say to themselves, 'I *must* get some sleep tonight; I'm so tired' — and, of course, because they are so anxious to sleep, they create sufficient inner tension to keep them awake.

A few nights of such programming and you have the problem of insomnia. The longer the situation continues, the greater the problem appears to be and the more difficult the pattern is to break. By means of hypnotherapy, however, the anxiety and tension can be dispelled, and sufficient relaxation induced for sleep to come again.

NAIL-BITING

Although children often bite their nails, it is a habit which usually vanishes as they become adults, and is therefore not normally considered worthy of treatment unless it persists into adult life. Most adults who bite their nails feel self-conscious and ashamed, even guilty, about doing it. And of course this worry feeds on itself — the more anxious they are about it, the more likely they are to continue the habit.

Treatment, which is normally successful, usually consists of a combination of approaches, from the elimination of anxiety, through the building up of confidence and pride in oneself, to the satisfying feeling of success and achievement as the nails at last begin to grow.

STAMMERING

Stammering is usually caused by fear during childhood. Sometimes the child may have had one frightening experience; sometimes it may result from prolonged fear of a particular person — usually a figure of authority such as a parent or a teacher.

Martin had stammered for as long he could remember. He was 43 when I first met him. He could not consciously recall when and how the stammer had begun. It had distressed him considerably during his childhood and teenage years; worried him a little less as he grew older; but now, as his progress in the company for which he worked brought him into contact with more and more people, he was anxious to eliminate it.

Martin agreed to be regressed to try and discover the initial cause of the stammer. Eventually he returned to the time when he was three years of age, and his grandfather, a retired military man, had been visiting the family. Martin had felt in awe of this large man with the authoritarian manner and very loud voice, and as a result had become tongue-tied and very shy; when questioned about day-to-day matters, he would hang his head and say nothing.

One day his grandfather was so exasperated by this that he picked up the child and shook him quite violently. Terrified, Martin had tried to answer the questions, but because of the vehemence with which he was being shaken, the words were stilted and incoherent.

This only further irritated his grandfather who put him down and walked away in disgust.

The adult Martin, on understanding this situation, was quite relieved. It proved to him that his stammering was not an inherent fault in his make-up, but was caused by a foolish and irascible old man — long since dead — who had had insufficient patience with a nervous child. In conjunction with a little practice by Martin in the privacy of his own home, this knowledge in itself went a long way towards curing the stammer.

Your stammer can be cured relatively easily through hypnosis if you are able to do any of the following without stammering:
- whisper;
- sing;
- speak aloud when alone.

Treatment will often involve patients, while in the

relaxed hypnotic state, being required to repeat words spoken by their therapist. A combination of words will be used with which the patients normally have difficulty, together with those which do not appear to cause any particular problem. Later, they will also be required to repeat whole phrases and sentences, and later still to discuss trivial subjects with the therapist, while still in a hypnotic trance.

Once they can do all of these things under hypnosis — and because they will be able to hear themselves doing it — the transition to being able to speak normally under ordinary circumstances is usually comparatively easy.

BLUSHING

Blushing usually occurs in people who, by disposition, are tense and nervous. Naturally, the moment they feel themselves beginning to blush — and are embarrassed by that feeling — they become more tense, thereby further increasing the tendency to blush. It is very significant that blushing tends to occur only on those parts of the body which can easily be seen by others — the neck and the face — and not on the hidden parts of the body.

General treatment for overcoming nervousness and improving confidence will usually put an end to this uncomfortable and, for the sufferer, embarrassing habit.

INFERTILITY

While the number of very young girls who become unintentionally pregnant is on the increase, so too is the number of women who desperately long to start a family but who have difficulty in conceiving. Obviously, in certain cases this is due to some physical cause on the part of either the husband or the wife. But the fact remains that there are many childless couples whose lack of ability to conceive cannot be explained in physical terms. In such cases, hypnotherapy can often provide the answer.

Over the years, an ever increasing number of women have consulted me for help in this matter — many of them on the advice of their doctors, when all else appears to have failed. Naturally, before even commencing treatment, I need to be assured that there is no physical reason for the couple's childlessness, and that all the relevant tests have been performed on both husband and wife.

Once we have ruled out any physical malfunction, we have to concentrate on the emotional aspect. The would-be mother is caught up in a vicious circle. Stress and anxiety probably caused the conception difficulties in the first place, and the longer those difficulties continue, the greater the anxiety becomes — particularly in the case of a woman in her thirties, who is very conscious of the fact that her fertile years are slipping away at what can seem an alarming rate. It is the task of the hypnotherapist to free her from the treadmill of depression, stress and anxiety by teaching her forms of relaxation. These may be deeper than those used in the treatment of other problems — although never so deep that she becomes unaware of what is being said.

My usual practice is to see a patient at weekly intervals for about a month, and then once a month for a further three or four months, during which time I teach her self-hypnosis. I would not normally expect a woman to conceive during the period when she is undergoing treatment — although I have been pleasantly surprised on more than one occasion. Once treatment has ended, the patient would have to continue with self-hypnosis, and it can then take anything from six months to a year for conception to occur.

If the woman does not become pregnant within that twelve-month period, it quite often indicates that she is not likely to do so at all without undergoing further treatment of a different nature. Although hypnotherapy does achieve a very high success rate when dealing with emotional infertility, it would be wrong to assume that conception automatically follows in every case.

IMPOTENCE

Impotence is a problem that can be helped by hypnotherapy, but the therapist is not often given the opportunity to prove it. Many men find it difficult and embarrassing even to arrange the initial consultation — although, perhaps surprisingly, discussions with professional colleagues indicate that such men find it easier to discuss their problem with a female therapist rather than a male one. Once they have taken that first step, however, the vast majority of men find a relatively speedy end to their anxieties. (Naturally, I am not discussing here those forms of impotence which have a purely physical cause, but only those which have an emotional base.)

Carl is a typical example. A successful businessman in his late forties, he had been married to Liza for 20 years and they had two teenage sons. Carl loved his wife and had no desire to be anything other than a faithful and caring husband.

One night Carl arrived home quite late after a professional function at which he had more to drink than usual — although he was by no means drunk. Liza was already in bed, though not asleep, and when Carl joined her he felt the desire to make love to his wife. Whether because he was tired or because of the amount of alcohol he had drunk, for the first time in his adult life Carl was unable to achieve an erection. This did not concern him too much at the time, but when he awoke next morning, he became acutely worried by what he considered his 'failure' of the night before. The next night, in Carl's own words, he had 'something to prove' and he began to make sexual advances to his wife — advances which once again culminated in his failure to achieve the desired erection.

And so it continued. Carl came to look upon his sexual relationship with Liza as a challenge rather than as a natural demonstration of their love and desire for one another. Every time he attempted to 'prove himself', he went into a state of such tension and anxiety that the attempt was doomed to failure from the start. By the time he consulted me, Carl had convinced himself that he was a sexual has-been, and that this side of his life with Liza was effectively over.

CARL CAME TO LOOK UPON HIS SEXUAL RELATIONSHIP WITH LIZA AS A CHALLENGE ....

What had happened to Carl happens to many men, particularly those in the 45-55 age group. A combination of tiredness and outside pressures, and frequently also alcohol, can result in any man not being capable of sexual intercourse on one particular occasion. As long as the man is able to put the situation into perspective and to see it for what it is — an unimportant incident which has no bearing on past or future ability — no other problems will follow.

It is only when that man experiences sexual desire on some future occasion, and is so anxious not to fail, that the very anxiety he feels may in fact bring about the dreaded failure. From then on, of course, he is trapped in a downward spiral. The next time he is faced with the same situation, he has *two* failures to build on. And so it goes from bad to worse, until he convinces himself that his impotence is with him for the rest of his life.

The first time I met Carl, we had a long discussion about his life in general. He recognized that he was under considerable pressure because of his business concerns, but felt that he could cope with this pressure as long as his marriage and home life were stable. Although Liza had assured him on several occasions that she was not troubled by his sexual inability, which she sensibly regarded as temporary, Carl was convinced that if the situation continued, he would lose the wife he loved so dearly. As a result he became more and more anxious, thereby increasing the pressures which surrounded him.

When I explained to Carl that I intended first to concentrate on teaching him how to achieve a state of deep relaxation under hypnosis, he was somewhat disappointed that I was not immediately tackling what to him was the most important problem. However, he was eventually able to accept that since the situation had already existed for several months, one week more would make little difference. And, of course, had he not spent that first week reinforcing his ability to relax and rid himself of external pressures, even for short periods of time, later success would have been much harder to achieve.

On his next visit, I once again hypnotized Carl, went through the relaxation technique with him, and then asked him to visualize himself in bed with his wife, making love to her joyously and successfully. As usual I instructed him to practise at home what he had done during the session — but in his mind only. Although loving physical contact with Liza was a good thing, he should not attempt to have actual sexual intercourse with her in that time. (I should point out here that Liza knew all about his visits to me, and was anxious to cooperate with the treatment in every way.)

The identical treatment was repeated on Carl's next visit to me, and again he was asked to refrain from actual intercourse with his wife, although once more being reminded that physical demonstrations of affection such as kissing, touching, caressing, were to be encouraged.

Five days after this visit, I received a telephone call from an ecstatic Carl. He and Liza had been lying in bed together the previous evening when, filled with desire for his wife, he had been unable to restrain himself and had made love to her as completely and successfully as he had always done in the past. His desire had been so great that he had not even stopped to worry about his earlier impotence and whether it had permanently affected him. He had broken out of the negative spiral in which he had been trapped. He was a happy man.

7.
PAIN AND ILLNESS

It is a relatively simple matter to take away pain by means of hypnosis, but this is a tool which must be carefully handled. Pain is present as a message to signal that something is wrong in the functioning of the body. A headache can be just that — but it can also indicate that the eyes need testing or even, in extreme cases, that a brain tumour exists.

Before you ask a hypnotherapist to assist with the removal of pain, it is essential that you consult an expert who can tell you whether the pain has any physical cause or whether it is trying to give you some sort of warning, and whether any medical treatment is necessary. If a new patient asks me to remove a nagging pain, I need either to speak to, or have a letter from, the patient's G.P. I want to be reassured that:

- the patient has been examined and no physical cause for the pain has been discovered;
- there *is* a physical cause which is being treated but that it would be quite safe for the pain to be removed.

Even when pain does have a known physical cause, it is a fact that the more anxious patients are, the more pain they will experience. Hypnotherapy makes it possible to reduce the anxiety and thereby relieve the pain. It is also possible to induce analgesia and anaesthesia; and this, in conjunction with the lower level of anxiety, can be sufficient to remove pain altogether.

I do not limit my remarks here to pain which has a physical cause. Psychosomatic pain is just as real to the sufferer. It brings with it the added problem that the sufferer often feels either foolish or guilty for having such pain. Even in this so-called enlightened age, many people are told by doctors, friends and relatives: 'There is nothing wrong with you. Pull yourself together and forget about the pain.' Psychosomatic pain is, in fact, just as real as any other, even though it may have been put there by the mind rather than the body.

PAIN WITH A PHYSICAL CAUSE

Victor was a man in his late fifties. When he came to see me some time ago, he was already having treatment from an osteopath for chronic back pain. The discs in his spine had apparently been eroded, and this was causing the severe pain he was feeling. While the osteopathic treatment would eventually alleviate the problem, there had been some permanent damage to his spine and so a complete 'cure' was not possible.

Victor understood his problem well, understood the treatment he was having and what the final outcome was likely to be. His main concern was that because of the constant pain in his back, he was unable to sleep at night. He felt he could cope with the daytime problems if only he could get a good night's sleep, but this was impossible. When I saw him for the first time, all he asked was to be taught some technique which would remove the pain at night and thus allow him to sleep and to wake refreshed, mentally if not always physically, the following day.

I spoke to Victor's osteopath on the 'phone to confirm that I would not, in fact, be adding to Victor's problems if I removed the night-time pain. I was assured that no harm could be done by this. So, with the osteopath's blessing, I proceeded to teach Victor through hypnosis how to achieve a numbness in the area of his back which was painful. This technique, combined with a deep relaxation therapy for general release of tension, was eventually sufficient to allow Victor to sleep well and deeply at night.

There are various possible methods to treat pain which has a known physical cause. It is always essential to begin by teaching patients how to relax. They can then be taught a form of self-hypnosis which will enable them to deal with the pain whenever they wish.

A feeling of numbness can be produced in the painful area by means of hypnosis and, once the therapist has done this, patients are given a post-hypnotic suggestion which enables them to do it for themselves. Sometimes this numbness is induced by 'freezing' the painful area, that is, by imagining that the area is growing colder and colder until it is actually numbed.

At other times I use misdirection. This is not unlike the technique frequently employed by stage magicians, who will ensure that the attention of the audience is focussed on some brightly lit part of the stage, so that the performer's sleight of hand will not be noticed. If you have a painful arm, for example, it is possible while you are in the hypnotic state to focus all your attention on your foot, your jaw or any other part of your anatomy. You must concentrate on this pain-free area, feeling it and being aware of it in great detail — what it looks like, what it feels like. While you are doing this, the suggestion will be directed to your subconscious mind that you are unaware of the pain in your arm.

PSYCHOSOMATIC PAIN

This is a pain which the mind has put there to cover some deep emotional feeling with which it cannot cope. Emotions most likely to cause such pain are:

Anger: If there is suppressed anger, whether towards another individual or towards fate, the person concerned will often suffer pain in some part of the body. For example, a man who has a tyrannical employer but who is unable, for the sake of his livelihood and his family, to stand up to him, may well develop pains or illnesses which make it impossible for him to go to work.

Anxiety: Pain will often develop when someone is faced with a situation which appears hopeless and from which there seems no escape.

Shame: There are still many people who feel ashamed about suffering from a depressive illness. Their subconscious mind will actually 'create' a physical pain, believing that this is much more likely to be understood by others.

Need for attention: Lonely people, and those who feel that they lack love and affection, may develop physical pains in order to gain the attention they feel they need.

Guilt: Vivienne was walking home one day from the local shops with her two small sons. She had a slight sore throat, all that remained of a cold from which she had been suffering earlier in the week. Her younger child, a boy of three, began to whine, saying that he wanted to be carried. Somewhat irritably Vivienne snapped at him, and told him that he was quite capable of walking the short distance home. Moments later the child tripped and cut his head badly on a paving stone. Vivienne felt consumed with guilt — if she had carried the child when asked, the accident would not have happened.

The boy's wound healed quite quickly, as children's wounds are wont to do. But some months later, Vivienne's throat was still painful. No physical cause for the pain could be found — and the cold had certainly long since disappeared. In fact, it was not until Vivienne was hypnotized, and was able to recall the incident concerning her son, that any connection was made between the child's fall and her chronic throat condition. Even though the sore throat had played no part in the original mishap, the two were connected in Vivienne's mind, and she had punished herself for months for 'allowing' her child to hurt himself.

Once she realized the cause of the problem, Vivienne could re-experience it under hypnosis. During the period of relaxation, she was able to see that what had happened was just an accident and not her fault. She made the proper connection between her sore throat on that day and the guilt she had felt when her son had fallen, and so corrected the mistaken image she had been carrying around in her subconscious mind for months.

Fear: Fear can have a logical or an illogical cause. Moira was sent to see me by her own doctor. She was a young Irish Roman Catholic woman in her late twenties. She had been married for two years, and for the greater part of that time had been having what she called her 'attacks'. These took the form of pains in the chest which made breathing difficult, dizziness, and on occasions even fainting. She never knew when the attacks would come, and had no control over them when they did. She had been examined, X-rayed, prodded and probed, but no physical cause for these periods of anxiety could be found.

The greatest problem for Moira was that she was desperate to start a family. She was the youngest of a family of eight children, and she had always hoped to have a large family herself. She was now frightened to become pregnant in case she had an attack which made her pass out, and fall and hurt the unborn child. Even if she survived the pregnancy without difficulty, she was afraid that she would have an attack while she was carrying the young child in her arms, and that she would drop it or do it some physical damage. Added tension was caused by members of her family, who kept dropping obvious hints and asking questions about when she was going to have children.

When I first met Moira, we had a long talk about her early life and her family in Ireland. It seemed likely that since there appeared to be no physical cause for her anxiety attacks, the solution to the mystery lay somewhere in her early life. I asked Moira whether she would be prepared to be regressed to see if we could discover any clues. She readily agreed to this, as she had happy memories of her childhood in the green countryside

of southern Ireland, with a large and boisterous family of brothers and sisters, all of whom tended to spoil her.

Regression to childhood is a fascinating process. The adult subject 'becomes' the child and will speak with a child's vocabulary. If asked to write, the adult will write as a child does, in large scrawled handwriting. I took Moira backwards from the age of about nine, and for a long while it seemed as though we were getting nowhere. Eventually we reached the time when Moira was just five years old. Under hypnosis she was able to recall a conversation with her mother:

'Why didn't you have any more babies after me? I wish I had a baby brother or sister to play with. Can I have one please?'

'No, Moira, I'm not going to have any more children.'

'Why not?'

'Good gracious, child, what would I be doing with more of you? And didn't it nearly kill me having you?'

This conversation had long since been forgotten by Moira, and presumably by her mother too. After all, it was of little or no significance to either of them. And yet that one phrase, 'didn't it nearly kill me having you?' — a phrase which so many women use, but which is rarely the literal truth — had been the cause of all Moira's problems later in life.

Far from being afraid that her attacks would do some damage during the course of a pregnancy, those attacks were, in fact, an ideal excuse for Moira not to become pregnant. Her subconscious mind had latched on to those unthinking words spoken all those years ago, and had allowed them to grow into an actual terror of childbirth and pregnancy. As a devout Catholic, Moira felt duty-bound to have children; to prevent this happening and yet not to interfere with her religious beliefs, her mind had 'created' her illness. She was therefore able to tell both herself and the world at large that she could not possibly become pregnant while these attacks persisted, and was also able to convince herself and the world at large that this decision was entirely for the good of any children she might conceive.

I would like to be able to say that once Moira understood the cause of the problem, the attacks immediately ceased and she eventually had a large family. Unfortunately, the world is not made up of such fairy-tale happy endings. What did happen in fact was that, with the help of hypnosis and counselling, Moria eventually came to terms with the problem. The attacks gradually subsided, and finally disappeared altogether. Whether in the end she had a family or not, I do not know. By the time her treatment had been completed, that possibility made her slightly nervous, but no longer terrified.

HYPNOSIS AND DENTISTRY

For many people a visit to the dentist is both painful and traumatic. Many never consult a dentist on a regular basis, sometimes preferring even to put up with a constant toothache rather than pay a visit, so great is their fear. When the time eventually comes when they can no longer bear the pain and they make a dental appointment, there are then the agonies of anticipatory fear, the stress and tension, both physical and mental, and the anxiety as to what the dentist will have to do and how long the suffering is likely to last.

Despite the fact that dental treatment today is extremely effective, and dentists are trained to do all that they can to preserve and protect teeth rather than to extract them — and to do this as painlessly as possible — nevertheless, it is sad but true that many people actually put off dental visits for so long that their teeth are past saving by the time they actually go for treatment.

IT IS A SAD BUT TRUE FACT THAT MANY PEOPLE PUT OFF THEIR VISITS TO A DENTIST FOR SO LONG THAT THEIR TEETH ARE PAST SAVING BY THE TIME THEY ACTUALLY GO FOR TREATMENT.

Hypnosis can assist in dentistry to a very great extent; in fact some dentists have actually taken formal training in hypnotherapy so that they can treat their own patients. Some of the ways in which hypnosis can help include:

Anticipation: Patients are taught self-hypnosis so that they can practise this at home as a form of deep relaxation, while at the same time contemplating their forthcoming visit to the dentist. In this way, they become accustomed to the idea of the dental visit being accompanied by feelings of peace and relaxation.
Treatment: It is a proven fact that anxiety or tension will increase the amount of pain experienced. Patients who are able to use their knowledge of self-hypnosis to

reduce the anxiety and tension they are experiencing will actually suffer less pain than they would otherwise have done.

Healing: Several dentists have noticed that when patients have been hypnotized for their treatment, any wounds caused by extraction bleed far less than would be the case with a non-hypnotized patient, and also that the wound itself appears to heal far more quickly.

CHILDBIRTH

This is another situation in which it is helpful if the patient can learn self-hypnosis — since neither I nor the majority of hypnotherapists would relish the idea of turning out at some unearthly hour to accompany a mother-to-be to the hospital labour-ward. Nor, I should imagine, would any busy hospital be keen to encourage such a practice. Many women now learn self-hypnosis as a matter of course, just as they automatically attend ante-natal clinics to be taught physical exercises.

The use of self-hypnosis to achieve deep relaxation during the course of pregnancy brings great benefits to both mother and unborn child. As well as the bliss of true physical relaxation, the period spent each day practising self-hypnosis provides a very special quiet period for mother and baby to be at peace with one another, and to become aware of each other in the most gentle of ways.

Patients who use self-hypnosis during the actual birth itself are far less likely to suffer painful tearing when the baby is born, and they are also more able to control both pain and natural anxiety during labour. Hypnosis can enable mothers to experience natural childbirth without the physical pain which often accompanies it.

One of my patients recently wrote to me: 'I wish I had known about self-hypnosis when I had my two sons. The first time I was so frightened and so tense that eventually I had to have a Caesarian section which was both painful and upsetting. The second time I was given so much of the gas and air mixture that I did not really know what was happening at all. It was all a sort of dream. But this time, when my little daughter was born, I was fully aware of all that was happening, while at the same time being quite relaxed and free from anything more than slight discomfort. Thank you.'

HIGH BLOOD-PRESSURE

In experiments, the blood-pressure of a patient has been measured immediately before and immediately after hypnosis. The results show that it is possible to bring the blood-pressure down considerably in a single session. Although this is not curing the problem which causes the high blood-pressure in the first place — indeed, it is often impossible for hypnosis to do this as high blood-pressure may well have a physical cause — it does help to alleviate both the symptoms and the dangers.

In cases where the patient's blood-pressure soars at times of stress and tension, then of course hypnotherapy can be of even greater help. Having taught the patient how to lower his or her blood-pressure, the therapist can then deal with the anxiety problems by means of hypnosis too.

MIGRAINE

There are two main types of migraine. One is caused by an actual allergy, usually to some substance such as cheese, wine or chocolate. Clearly, here, the only effective treatment is to avoid eating or drinking whatever it is which brings on the migraine attack.

The other and more common cause of migraine is tension. When helping a migraine sufferer, there are, therefore, two stages in the hypnotic treatment. The first is to teach the patient how to make the migraine disappear before it really takes hold. All migraine sufferers know when an attack is about to strike — they can feel it coming on. That is the time to stop whatever they are doing for a space of some 15 or 20 minutes, and to find a quiet spot where they can practise the self-hypnosis they have been taught. This will have the effect of making the pain disappear before it reaches anything like its usual severity. Since it is physically impossible for someone to be totally relaxed and at the same time to suffer a tension headache of any sort, the sensation of deep relaxation brought about by the hypnosis will effectively remove the pain of the migraine.

ALL MIGRAINE SUFFERERS KNOW WHEN AN ATTACK IS ABOUT TO STRIKE ..

The second stage of treatment involves the therapist working with the migraine sufferer to discover where possible the reason for the tension, and to help alleviate the stress caused.

ASTHMA

Asthma is treated in very much the same way as migraine. Most cases of true asthma are emotionally based. This makes it very different from complaints such as hay fever, where one is dealing with a physical allergy to things like dust, pollen or chemicals. It is often not possible to regress the patient to discover the source of the asthma, since this is frequently lodged somewhere in very early childhood — it can even be the trauma of the birth itself. Some experts believe that asthma may be caused in an unborn child by the extreme tension of the mother, but

117

this has not yet been satisfactorily proved.

Having established that the patient is indeed suffering from emotionally based asthma, and not from some physical allergy, the treatment proceeds in much the same way as for migraine. As with a migraine sufferer, the asthmatic always knows when an attack is about to begin. Usually this very knowledge results in feelings of terror and panic — an anticipatory fear of not being able to breathe, and of unbearable pressure in the chest.

As a first stage the hypnotherapist with asthmatic patients usually teaches them self-hypnosis so that, whenever an attack threatens, they are able to make it recede by themselves. It is amazing how often the mere knowledge of this ability is enough to reduce the actual number of attacks suffered. The fact that patients know they need never again suffer the miseries of a full-scale attack helps to develop their confidence and their self-assurance. It is then up to the hypnotherapist to build on this new confidence to help them become less emotional and anxious.

The success rate for those suffering from either migraine or asthma is very high indeed.

CANCER

At one time it was believed that all cancer had a purely physical cause. We now know that this is not so. Naturally, there are some cases where the cause of the cancer is known to be physical — the person who has smoked 60 cigarettes a day for 40 years, for example, or someone who has worked without proper protection in close contact with chemically abrasive substances. Should such people develop cancer later in life, the reason can be well understood.

There are, however, many cases where cancer has been brought about by the mind rather than the body. If we were to go back two or three years in the life of every cancer sufferer, quite often we would come to some traumatic incident with which the person had been unable to cope. Perhaps there was a sudden bereavement, an unexpected divorce, redundancy for a man who feels that he is too old to get another job. This does not for one moment imply that everyone who suffers a shock like that is going to develop cancer within the next two or three years. Of course that is not so. But, in certain cases, the body will react where the mind is unable to cope.

Hypnotherapy can and does help people to overcome cancer. It cannot take the place of conventional treatment but, used in conjunction with it, the power of the human mind can work what appear to be miracles.

Leaders in this field are O. Carl Simonton, MD, DABR, and his wife, Stephanie Matthews-Simonton. This eminent husband-and-wife team, consisting of a radiation oncologist and a psychotherapist, have been running the Cancer Counselling and Research Center in Dallas, Texas, for many years. They combine a programme of diet, exercise and hypnosis using visualization, together with whatever medical treatment may be considered necessary — with astounding results. The newsletter of the Association of Humanistic Psychology said of them:

'Compared to US national averages, the Simontons' "terminally ill" patients have lived longer — in some cases experiencing dramatic remissions — and functioned more fully than typical cancer patients ... In the burgeoning field of holistic health practice, [the Simontons] are bold and level-headed pioneers.'

In his book *Getting Well Again* (published by Bantam) O. Carl Simonton describes the value of the relaxation and mental imagery techniques (which can be taught through hypnosis) in this way:

'The list below contains some of the benefits of the relaxation/mental imagery process.
1. The process can decrease fear. Most fear comes from feeling out of control — in the case of cancer, feeling that your body is deteriorating and you are powerless.

Relaxation and mental imagery help you to see your role in regaining health so that you begin to sense your own control.

2. The process can bring about attitude changes and strengthen the "will to live".

3. It can effect physical changes, enhancing the immune system and altering the course of a malignancy. Since mental processes have a direct influence on the immune system and hormonal balances in the body, physical changes can be directly attributed to changes in thought patterns.

4. The process can serve as a method for evaluating current beliefs and altering those beliefs, if desired. Alterations in the symbols and pictures that you use can dynamically alter beliefs to those more compatible with health.

5. The process can be a tool for communicating with the unconscious — where many of our beliefs are at least partially buried.

6. It can be a general tool for decreasing tension and stress and have a significant effect on underlying body functions.

7. The process can be used to confront and alter the stance of hopelessness and helplessness. We have seen again and again how this underlying depression is a significant factor in the development of cancer. As people begin to picture their bodies regaining health, and with it their ability to solve the problems that existed prior to the malignancy, they weaken their sense of helplessness and hopelessness. Indeed, as the patients proceed toward health, they gain a sense of confidence and optimism.'

Some time ago, when I was living in London, I worked with a cancer self-help group, with the knowledge and consent of the physicians involved. This group consisted of nine women whose ages ranged from 22 to 74 years. They had various forms of cancer for which they were receiving treatment at one of the London teaching

THE RELAXATION/MENTAL IMAGERY PROCESS CAN BE USED TO CONFRONT AND ALTER THE STANCE OF HOPELESSNESS AND HELPLESSNESS.

hospitals, but each woman had in addition decided that she was going to work to improve and prolong her own life. As well as teaching the patients self-hypnosis so that they could work on themselves in their own homes, I used to see them once a week for a group discussion and hypnotherapy session.

Of the nine patients, three had prolonged periods of remission, and three actually had a reduction (in one case a complete disappearance) of the growth as shown on their X-rays. The credit for this must go to the patients themselves. All I could do was to teach them the techniques; the effort, determination and hard work were all theirs.

I am not suggesting here that all cancer patients will necessarily respond in this way to holistic treatment. But there have been sufficient cases to make this a very worthwhile form of therapy, and the increasing number of Cancer Help Centres and Clinics only underlines our growing belief in the effectiveness of mind over body in such situations.

8.
FURTHER INFORMATION

Having learned a little about hypnotherapy — what it is and how it is used — you may be interested to find out more. The next few pages are intended to help you in your search. You will find details of other books to read, of organizations who can supply you with lists of practitioners in your area, and of cassettes, courses and other aids which are available.

FURTHER READING

Hypnosis — A Gateway to Better Health
by Brian Roet (Weidenfeld and Nicolson, 1986).
An interesting book written for the prospective patient in a humorous, chatty style.

The Inner Source — Exploring Hypnosis
by Dr Herbert Spiegel (Holt, Reinhart & Winston, 1984).
An informative and inspiring work.

Hypnosis — Its Nature and Therapeutic Uses
by H.B. Gibson (Taplinger Publishing Co., New York, 1977).
A factual book about hypnosis by a Professor of Psychology who teaches and researches the subject.

Hypnosis
by David Waxman (Unwin, 1981).
A clear and reliable guide for both patients and practitioners.

Self-Improvement Through Self-Hypnosis
by R.N. Shrout (Thorsons, 1985).
A guide to self-hypnosis, positive thinking and auto-
suggestion.

Hypnotism and the Power Within
by S.J. Van Pelt (Skeffington & Sons, 1950).
A book which is slightly dated in style but whose theories
and ideas are still valid and interesting.

Getting Well Again
by O. Carl Simonton, Stephanie Matthews-Simonton and
James L. Creighton (Bantam Books, 1978).
Details about the work of the Simontons, and a guide to
overcoming cancer for patients and their families.

Hypnosis Regression Therapy
by Ursula Markham (Piatkus, 1991).
How reliving early experiences can help you
improve your life.

Holistic Living
by Dr Patrick Pietroni (J.M. Dent, 1986).
Patrick Pietroni is Chairman of the British Holistic
Medical Association. His book deals with all aspects of
holism and contains interesting chapters on stress,
relaxation, and understanding your mind.

Open the Window
by Joan Gibson (Gateway Books, 1985).
Practical suggestions to help those suffering from
depression.

Psycho-Cybernetics
by Maxwell Maltz (Wilshire Book Company, 1960).
and *The Magic Power of Self-Image Psychology*
by Maxwell Maltz (Pocket Books, New York, 1964).
Two fascinating books dealing with the power of the
human mind.

Regression Therapy using Hypnosis
by Ursula Markham (Piatkus Books, 1991)
About regression therapy and how it can be used in the
treatment of deep-rooted problems, helping you to
access and come to terms with traumatic emotional
experiences from your past.

The Elements of Visualisation
by Ursula Markham (Elements Books, 1990)
Visualisation is a technique for using the imagination in
a creative and positive way to bring about desired
changes within ourselves and so within our lives.

Creating a Positive Self-Image
by Ursula Markham (Element Books, 1995)
Showing how the special technique of Hypnothink can
bring self-confidence, success and happiness within your
reach.

USEFUL ADDRESSES

Societies and organizations where you can obtain
further information about hypnosis, and also lists of
practitioners. Please supply a stamped addressed
envelope.

British Holistic Medical Association.
179 Gloucester Place
London NW1 6DX

Council for Complementary and Alternative Medicine
Suite 1, 19a Cavendish Square
London W1M 9AD

British Society for Medical and Dental Hypnosis
42 Links Road
Ashstead, Surrey KT21 2HJ

(Scottish Branch)
342 Kilmarnock Road
Glasgow G43 2DQ

British Society for Experimental and Clinical Hypnosis
PO Box 133
Canterbury
Kent

Hypnotherapy Register
The Hypnothink Foundation
PO Box 66
Glocester GL2 9YG

British Assn. for Therapeutical Hypnosis
13 Deepdene Court, 8 Kingswood Road
Shortlands, Bromley
Kent BR2 0NW

Australia

Australian Society of Hypnosis
PO Box 366
Glenleg
South Australia 5045

Australian Society for Clincal and Experimental
Hypnosis
Royal Melbourne Hospital
Royal Parade
Parkville
Victoria

Canada

Ontario Society for Clincal Hypnosis
170 St George Street, Ste 1001
Toronto, Ontario

United States

American Association of Professional Hypnotherapists
PO Box 29
Boones Mill
VA 24065
United States

Courses in hypnotherapy and allied subjects:

The Hypnothink Foundation
PO Box 66
Gloucester GL2 9YG

National College of Hypnosis and Psychotherapy
25 Market Square
Nelson
Lancashire BB9 7LP

School of Hypnosis and Advanced Psycotherapy
28 Finsbury Park Road
London N4 2JX

Proudfoot School of Hypnosis and Psychotherapy
9 Belvedere Park
Scarborough
North Yorkshire YO11 2QX

British Assn. for Therapeutical Hypnosis
13 Deepedene Court
Kingswood Road
Shortlands, Bromley
Kent BR2 0NW

Cassettes on hypnosis and self-hypnosis can be obtained from:

The Hypnothink Foundation
PO Box 66
Gloucester GL2 9YH

Breese Publications
164 Kensington Park Road
London W11 2ER

Write for full details, enclosing a stamped addressed
envelope.

To order your copy direct from Vermilion, use the form below or call TBS DIRECT on **01621 819596**.

Please send me

...... copies of **MEDITATION** @ £6.99 each
...... copies of **ACUPUNCTURE** @ £6.99 each
...... copies of **COLOUR HEALING** @ £7.99 each
...... copies of **ALEXANDER TECHNIQUE** @ £6.99 each
...... copies of **AROMATHERAPY** @ £6.99 each
...... copies of **BATES METHOD** @ £7.99 each
...... copies of **REFLEXOLOGY** @ £5.99
...... copies of **IRIDOLOGY** @ £8.99 each
...... copies of **MASSAGE THERAPY** @ £7.99

Mr/Ms/Mrs/Miss/Other (Block Letters)

....

Address...

....

....

Postcode....................Signed................................

HOW TO PAY

☐ I enclose a cheque/postal order for
£......................... made payable to 'Tiptree Book Services'

☐ I wish to pay by Access/Visa/Switch/Delta card (delete where appropriate)

Card Number ☐☐☐☐☐☐☐☐☐☐☐☐☐☐☐☐

Expiry Date ☐☐☐☐

Post order to **TBS Direct, Tiptree Book Services, St. Lukes Chase, Tiptree, Essex, CO5 0SR.**